n.1

18.00

WHICH ROAD TO THE PAST?
TWO VIEWS OF HISTORY

ROBERT WILLIAM FOGEL AND G. R. ELTON

WHICH
ROAD
TO
THE
PAST?

TWO VIEWS OF HISTORY

YALE UNIVERSITY PRESS   NEW HAVEN AND LONDON

Published with assistance from the
foundation established in memory of
Philip Hamilton McMillan of the
Class of 1894, Yale College.

Designed by Sally Harris and set in Zapf International type.
Printed in the United States of America by Halliday Lithograph,
West Hanover, Massachusetts.

Library of Congress Cataloging in Publication Data

Fogel, Robert William.
  Which road to the past?

  Includes index.
    1. History—Methodology—Addresses, essays, lectures
  2. Historiography—Addresses, essays, lectures.
  3. History—Philosophy—Addresses, essays, lectures.
  I. Elton, G. R. (Geoffrey Rudolph) II. Title.
  D16.F69 1983   901   83-3573
  ISBN 0-300-03011-8
  ISBN 0-300-03278-1 (pbk.)

10   9   8   7   6   5   4   3   2

To Ep

CONTENTS

INTRODUCTION

Historians have taken to talking about what they supposedly do: discussions of methods, of theory, of orthodoxies and heresies reverberate through the common rooms, penetrate into the learned journals, and even fill whole books—usually little ones. In itself, this preoccupation, though it takes up time that might be given to actually writing history, has its virtues, especially in countering the well-meant attentions of learned nonhistorians. The problems and meaning of endeavors to rediscover the past have for some time formed a favorite theme for certain philosophers whose profound and original analyses do not always seem relevant to the working historian. This last, a fairly common creature, must nevertheless have become aware that his concerns are capable of being thought about philosophically, and it is beginning to worry him: is he missing out on something that would at long last make his labors respectable in the eyes of the deeper thinkers? By and large, the answer is no, but the stimulus provided by philosophers of history may yet turn the working historian into a thinking historian.

A recent example well illustrates what too often happens, and since it concerns itself with one of the present authors' special concerns—the nature and use of historical evidence—it merits a brief word. B. C. Hurst has explained that he has succeeded in demolishing what he calls "the myth" of this evidence and to give an account of it which he regards as analytically more accurate and as more fully descriptive of what historians in fact do.[1] Splendid: all the time that we

---

1. B. C. Hurst, "The Myth of Historical Evidence," *History and Theory* 20 (1981): 278–90.

and our colleagues have been reading, evaluating, and integrating evidence, a debate about its nature has apparently been going on among people doing none of this, two rival "models" of description have been produced, and both now turn out to be mythical. So far as we can see, so does the third model: they are all myths, which is to say, explanatory constructions devised by a priestly caste for the instructive bewilderment of the multitude. None of these investigations offers any help touching the complex processes involved in turning extant detail into historical reconstruction, and historians desirous of attending to exercises going on high above their heads seemingly have a choice of two reactions, neither very satisfactory. Either they ignore the philosophers and get on with what they are doing, but that might mean that they will continue to work without understanding how they are doing it. Or they down tools to listen to the philosophers, but this will most likely mean that tools will stay permanently downed. On the whole, it would seem better to apply the experience of using historical evidence to an understanding of the problems its existence poses, and we shall say a little about it here and there.

Our main concern, however, will be different. Among the current discussions, the impact of new and sophisticated methods in the study of the past occupies an important place. The new "scientific" or "cliometric" history—born of the marriage contracted between historical problems and advanced statistical analysis, with economic theory as bridesmaid and the computer as best man—has made tremendous advances in the last generation. It has acquired a large body of devoted followers who understandably claim great things for the mistress they serve and as understandably, though less excusably, would wish to see her dominate in all the teaching and research of historians. Naturally enough, the onrush of cliometricians has called forth some quite violent hostility from "traditionalists" who feel themselves threatened and react with emotional and wholesale condemnations. The debate has not always observed the courtesies proper to an exchange of views among scholars. Thus the time seems ripe for a dispassionate review of the basic question: can one define two separate species of history to be called scientific and traditional, and in what ways do the two differ?

We start from the proposition that if these two species exist they are both legitimate: we resist attitudes which would lead to wars of mutual extermination. To support our request to be heard we put forward no more than the fact that we have both written a good deal of history after coming to the task from the opposite ends of the supposed spectrum. Perhaps, since neither of us has the slightest inclination to doubt the other's claim to be a true historian, we lack an essential qualification for doing battle, at least in the eyes of those for whom argument means conflict. Indeed, we have to admit that despite our very different points of departure we agree on these topics far more than we disagree, to the point where the reader may come to suspect collusion. After all, what can be more frustrating than having to listen to a series of approving slaps upon two backs which one had hoped to see pierced by daggers concealed in the slapping hands? We recall an occasion at Newnham College, Cambridge, when a vastly overcrowded lecture room, full of people come to witness a fight to the death between King Kong and the Giant Lizard, grew more and more restive as it listened to two woolly lambs peacefully lying down side by side. Well, we cannot help it: there will be no bloodbath. However, we very definitely remain distinguishable, and there are quite enough disagreements between us to produce a debate which we, at least, think interesting.

1 "SCIENTIFIC" HISTORY AND TRADITIONAL HISTORY

Robert William Fogel

Although in some respects the verbal clash between "scientific" and traditional historians is as loud as ever, the interpenetration of their opposing modes of research is now quite well advanced.* The long period of cultural warfare has turned some of the partisans into determined enemies, but they are few in number. The clash is not rooted in irreconcilable ideological positions or in territorial struggles, even though these may be involved incidentally. It turns on more subtle and more complicated differences over research agendas, methodology, and style. Reflection on the substance of these differences suggests that the affinities and complementarities between "scientific" and traditional historians are more important than the differences. Nearly a quarter of a century has elapsed since the revival of the conflict. Placing the points at issue in an historical perspective not only serves to clarify past events but also suggests the nature of the emerging synthesis.

*This is a revised version of the paper originally prepared for presentation at the Sixth International Congress of Logic, Methodology and Philosophy of Science and published in the proceedings of that congress: L. J. Cohen, J. Łoś, H. Pfeiffer and K. P. Podewski, eds., *Logic, Methodology, and Philosophy of Science, VI. Proceedings of the Sixth International Congress of Logic, Methodology and Philosophy of Science, Hannover 1979* (Amsterdam: North-Holland Publishing Co., 1982), pp. 15–61. In addition to the many helpful comments and criticisms acknowledged in the proceedings, I am indebted to W. Elliot Brownlee, Stanley L. Engerman, David Galenson, and Charles Kahn for suggestions on the revisions and to Douglass C. North, whose suggestions are reflected both in the revisions of this essay and in my contribution to the concluding essay.

The term "scientific" is intended to designate a large group of practicing historians in the United States and elsewhere who refer to themselves as "scientific," "social-scientific," or "cliometric" historians. "Scientific" appears in quotation marks whenever it is used to designate this group, partly in order to emphasize that the usurpation of the term is questioned by scholars outside of the group and partly to remove any moral advantage that might otherwise be attached to the term.

The Quest for Scientific History

By the early decades of the nineteenth century, if not sooner, it was clear that scientific and technological discoveries were radically transforming the mode of production and altering long-established habits of life. The Industrial Revolution was, on final analysis, the gift not of liberal kings and democratic politicians, but of practical men who saw how to transform these discoveries into new methods of production. In that incredible burst of inventive activity and entrepreneurship that did so much to transform the nations of Europe and North America, it seemed as if science had no bounds. During the first half of the nineteenth century space and time were conquered by steamboats, railroads, and telegraphs. The prices of one-time luxury commodities declined so rapidly that they were transformed into necessities, not only for the rich and the well-to-do, but also for the common people. And a wide array of commodities and services came into being or were popularized.

It was quite natural that those who pondered the nature of human affairs should have been deeply impressed by the transformation that resulted from the applications of science to production. If the application of science to production could transform industry, could not the application of science to social and political relationships transform these as well? The question was all the more urgent because Europe and America had already entered an age of social and political revolution and because long-standing ideologies were coming under increasing challenge. Stimulated by the thought of Enlightenment thinkers, Malthus sought the laws that governed the growth of populations; Ricardo sought the principles that governed the distribution of income; Morgan began the study of systems of kinship; and LePlay sought to establish regularities in the organization of families. From their work and the work of like-minded scholars, there arose such disciplines as economics, demography, anthropology, and sociology. From their work, as well as the work of biologists, there also arose a new subfield of mathematics called statistics. And the collectivity of these fields, which sought to use the methods of the natural sciences to study the social behavior of human beings and to derive lawlike statements that governed their behavior, became known as the social sciences.

History was also deeply influenced by the natural sciences, but the lines of influence were complex and somewhat contradictory. To some historians being scientific meant being objective, and objectivity required a rejection of conceptions of history that emanated from moral philosophy. Objectivity, as defined by Leopold von Ranke, required, above all, a deep immersion in the primary sources and the subjection of these sources to intense internal and external criticism. This quest for the authenticity of evidence, which involved techniques developed in classical philology, including paleography and diplomatics, led to the heavily footnoted monograph as the foundation of historical research. It also led to an emphasis on the unique and particularistic nature of history and to a rejection of the applicability of law or lawlike statements to the study of history.[1] As Charles H. Hull put it, "the ultimate units with which the historian deals are not atoms, or any sort of instrumental abstractions, whose individual differences may be ignored, but they are men and the deeds of men." Men and their deeds, he held, were "too complex and too

1. Recent discussions of Ranke's methodology and influence include Georg G. Iggers, "The Image of Ranke in American and German Historical Thoughts," *History and Theory* 2 (1962): 17–40; Peter Gay, *Style in History* (New York: Basic Books, 1974); Leonard Krieger, *Ranke: The Meaning of History* (Chicago: University of Chicago Press, 1977).

variously conditioned to be subject to the concept of general law."[2]

This is the point on which advocates of scientific history were most deeply divided. Many historians during the late nineteenth and early twentieth centuries, deeply influenced by the revolutionary discoveries in biology, especially the work of Darwin, and by the integration of biology with physics through the laws of thermodynamics, began to propound the view that "history represented a continuum with the universe of nature, and like nature, was . . . governed by law." In his presidential address to the American Historical Association, Henry Adams spoke with awe about the "immortality that would be achieved by the man who should successfully apply Darwin's methods to the facts of human history." Such a breakthrough seemed at hand to Adams, who contended that "four out of five serious students of history have in the course of their work, felt that they stood on the brink of a great generalization." That was in 1894. Fifteen years later, the breakthrough was yet to be achieved and no longer seemed imminent. When George Burton Adams delivered his presidential address he warned against efforts to discover "the forces that control society" or "to formulate the laws of their action," calling them "the allurements of speculation." "The field of the historian," he said, "is, and must long remain, the discovery and recording of what actually happened."[3]

2. Charles H. Hull, "The Service of Statistics to History," *Quarterly Publications of the American Statistical Association* 14 (1914): 35.

3. Edward Saveth, "Scientific History in America: Eclipse of an Idea," in *Essays in American Historiography*, ed. Donald Sheehan and Harold C. Syrett (New York: Columbia University Press, 1960), p. 4; Henry Adams, "The Tendency of History," *Annual Report of the American Historical Association* (1894): 19; George Burton Adams, "History and the Philosophy of History," *American Historical Review* 14 (1909): 236. The rise and decline of scientific history during the late nineteenth and early twentieth centuries are described in W. Stull Holt, "The Idea of Scientific History in America," *Journal of the*

And so the majority of the profession removed themselves from the effort to establish empirically warranted laws of human behavior and appeared content to leave such speculative enterprises to the social sciences. To some historically minded social scientists this seemed to be a reasonable division of labor. John William Burgess, for example, told historians that their task was the "true and faithful" recording of "the facts of human experience," and that political scientists would put these facts "into the form of propositions" or "principles" of political behavior.[4]

Historians, of course, generally refused to accept such a narrow definition of their function. Many economic historians, for example, still aimed to produce lawlike statements, not by the deductive process that animated Marshall and other economic theorists, but through an inductive process, which began with the systematic collection of the facts of economic history.[5] And if the main body of historians, concentrated largely in political history, gave up the search for behavioral laws per se, they did not give up looser and what seemed to them less pretentious forms of generalization.

The Triumph of Traditional History

The idea that there could be a special historical approach to the interconnection of facts was given systematic expression by Johann Gustav Droysen, who, drawing heavily from the work of Wilhelm von Humboldt, sought to define a process

---

History of Ideas 1 (1940): 352–62; Saveth, "Scientific History in America," pp. 1–19; John Higham et al., *History* (Englewood Cliffs: Prentice-Hall, 1965).

4. John W. Burgess, "Political Science and History," *Annual Report of the American Historical Association* (1896): 209–10.

5. See Robert W. Fogel, "The Reunification of Economic History with Economic Theory," *American Economic Review* 55 (1965): 92–98, and the sources cited there.

called *ideengeschichte*, or "imaginative understanding." As Jurgen Herbst summed it up, historical truth "consisted not only of facts but of ideas—invisible elements of history 'which relate the fragments to each other, put single phenomena in their proper perspective, give form to the whole.'" To "fuse the visible facts with the invisible ideas" required imagination. In exercising this imagination "the historian resembled the poet, except that it was the historian's special duty to subordinate his imagination to an absolute fidelity to past actualities."[6]

According to Droysen, historical thought was a well-defined "epistemological category" that was "distinct from those of the physical sciences and of speculative philosophy." Toward the end of the nineteenth century and early in the twentieth century philosophers such as Dilthey and Croce, and later Collingwood, sought to explore this new epistemological category and thus gave rise to the subfield called "the analytical philosophy of history." They held that historical agents could not be viewed as "mere pieces of observable 'behavior,' reducible to (or explicable in terms of) purely physical items." It followed that the "essential task of the historian is to 'rethink' or 're-enact' in his mind the deliberations of historical agents, thereby rendering intelligible the events with which he has to deal in a way that finds no parallel in the physical sciences."[7]

With such philosophical underpinning, historians tended to move further away from the notion that natural science provided a model for historical research. In America the climax of the process of disenchantment was probably reached in the 1930s with the presidential addresses of Carl Becker and Charles

6. Jurgen Herbst, *The German Historical School in American Scholarship* (Ithaca: Cornell University Press, 1965), pp. 108–09.

7. Ibid; see also Patrick Gardiner, "History: The Philosophy of History," in *International Encyclopedia of the Social Sciences* (New York: Macmillan, 1968), vol. 6, p. 430; cf. H. Stuart Hughes, *Consciousness and Society: The Reorientation of European Social Thought 1890–1930* (New York: Random House, 1958).

Beard, which Cushing Strout has described as a pragmatic revolt against scientific history and historical positivism. Becker and Beard denied that the "historian's account of the past" could be "genuine knowledge" except "to a very limited degree." An historical account, they argued, was "fundamentally a temporary appraisal, based on the historian's interests and values, which are themselves conditioned by his particular time, circumstances, and personality." While it cannot be said that the majority of historians adopted this view of their craft, many were influenced by it, and during the 1930s, 1940s, and early 1950s there was a continued weakening of the earlier identification with the natural sciences. This was true even in the collection and appraisal of evidence, and historians gradually shifted from the natural sciences to law as their model for the rigorous evaluation of evidence.[8]

The dominance of the legal model is quite evident in the standards for the appraisal of evidence set forth in the 1954 edition of the *Harvard Guide to American History*.[9] The Harvard historians first warned of the need to determine carefully the actual meaning of words in particular contexts. Some words have a drastically different meaning today than they did in the past, while other words, even at a given moment of time, have a different meaning for one group than for another. "Property," they pointed out, "meant one thing to John Locke, another to the American Liberty League." They also emphasized the need to be sensitive "to irony, satire, epigram, literary

8. Cushing Strout, *The Pragmatic Revolt in American History: Carl Becker and Charles Beard* (Ithaca: Cornell University Press, 1966), p. 9; cf. Higham, *History*, chaps. 3 and 4.
9. The quotations in this paragraph, including the indented quotation, and in the next one are from Oscar Handlin et al., *Harvard Guide to American History* (Cambridge: Harvard University Press, Belknap Press, 1954), pp. 24–25.

flourish, overstatement, understatement, and the whole human range of nuance, inflection, and exaggeration."

Once satisfied that he understands what the witness is saying, the historian must then consider whether the witness was in a position to know what he was talking about; then whether, if the witness was in that position, he had the skill and competence to observe accurately; then whether, if he knew the facts, he would be inclined to represent them fairly, or whether circumstances— emotional, intellectual, political—might incline him to emphasize some aspects of an episode and minimize others. Many motives, worthy and unworthy, deflect or distort observation: national patriotism, class conditioning, political partisanship, religious faith, moral principle, love, hate, and survival.

To get at the truth, the historian must cross-examine the witness. The Harvard historians provided sensible guides to this process. They pointed to the need to take account of the "general character" of each witness, but warned about "the logical fallacy of confusing the origin of the story with its value: the chronic liar may bear true witness on a particular occasion, and the high-minded man may get hopelessly muddled." They also warned about the "careless" errors in letters and the "premeditated" entries in diaries, about the faulty or self-serving recollections of aged men, and the easy acceptance of "poetic fancy . . . as historical fact." Because it "is all too easy to poison the bloodstream of history," they emphasized the need to find independent corroboration for any proffered fact.

Like treason in the Constitution, a historical fact ideally should rest "on the testimony of two witnesses to some overt act, or on confession in open court." But sometimes, alas, there is but a single witness; or, if there are two, and of equal competence and probity, their versions may be in head-on collision. Charles Evans Hughes told his biographer that he had recommended Robert H. Jackson as chief justice of the Supreme Court; President Truman's firm recollection is that Hughes recommended Fred M. Vinson; no documentary evidence survives: how to solve the insoluble conflict?

A judge and jury, indeed, would go mad if they had to decide cases on evidence which will often seem more than satisfactory to the historian. But there is no escape; the historian, if he is to interpret at all, will try and convict on evidence which a court would throw out as circumstantial or hearsay. The victims of the historical process have to seek their compensation in the fact that history provides them with a far more flexible appellate procedure. The historian's sentences are in a continuous condition of review; few of his verdicts are ever final.

I have dwelt on standards of evidence because it is central to the distinction between what I have called "traditional" history and the brand of "scientific" history that is now successfully challenging it. Before proceeding to a comparison of these two modes of historical research, it is first necessary to consider the subject matter of traditional history.

During the nineteenth century historical research, not only in the United States, but also in England, France, and Germany, was focused on politics. The words that Herbert Baxter Adams inscribed on the wall of his seminar are so famous now that they are a cliché: "History is Past Politics and Politics are Present History." The aphorism was not original with Adams, who took it from Edward A. Freeman. Nor was preoccupation with politics new. From the beginning of the craft, historians had focused on the state, the church, and other organs of power; and the authors often had been persons who held positions of power or were close to those who held them. During the era of the absolute rule by divine sovereigns, historians were often figures at court who sought to glorify the deeds of their patrons. After the onset of the age of revolution, politics continued to remain the focus of historical writing, but then the historians celebrated the accomplishments of the revolution and explained the reasons for the downfall of the old regime. The rise of scientific history in Germany and its subsequent spread through Europe and America further accentuated the emphasis on politics. For state papers were the most carefully preserved and easily accessible of the primary sources that Ranke and others had made quintessential.[10]

Early in the twentieth century strong movements developed in Europe and America for histories that included, but transcended, politics. The origins of these movements can be traced to such earlier scholars as Giambattista Vico, Lord Macaulay, and Jules Michelet, whose broader, more social conception of history represented an alternative to the dominant political tradition. A shift in the balance began to become evident about the time of World War I or shortly thereafter. In the United States James Harvey Robinson called for "a new history" that would embrace "every trace and vestige of everything that man has done or thought since first he appeared on the earth." Such history, he continued, would not only "follow the fate of nations" but also "depict the habits and emotions of the most obscure individual." In France the movement for

10. Herbert B. Adams, "Is History Past Politics?" *Johns Hopkins University Studies* 13 (1895): 67–81; Harry E. Barnes, *A History of Historical Writing*, 2d ed. rev. (New York: Dover Publications, 1962), chaps. 4–10; Arthur Marwick, *The Nature of History* (London: Macmillan, 1976), chap. 2.

"total history" revolved around the journal *Annales*. Perhaps more than any group in any other country, the *Annales* group eagerly drew upon the full array of ideas and approaches generated by the social sciences, including the development of a sociological approach to politics. They have also displayed great methodological flexibility, so much so that in recent years such prominent members of the group as Emmanuel Le Roy Ladurie and François Furet have been in the forefront of French scholars seeking to apply quantitative methods to the study of history. Collectively, the members of the *Annales* group have explored nearly the full range of approaches now practiced in the study of history, although some have a greater affinity to traditional approaches while others have a greater affinity to the new brand of "scientific" history.[11]

American historians were somewhat ambivalent regarding what they should or should not take from the social sciences. At first, economic ideas were the most easy to incorporate. Frederick Jackson Turner laid great emphasis on the effects of the vast supply of land in the shaping of American democracy;

11. James H. Robinson, *The New History: Essays Illustrating the Modern Outlook* (New York: Macmillan, 1912), p. 1. For discussions of the "new history," see Barnes, *History of Historical Writing*, pp. 330–402; Higham, *History*, esp. pp. 104–16, 255–67. For discussions of the *Annales* group, see Maurice Aymard, "The *Annales* and French Historiography (1929–72)," *The Journal of European Economic History* 1 (1972): 491–511; Bernard Bailyn, Review of *French Historical Method: The Annales Paradigm*, by Traian Stoianovich, *Journal of Economic History* 37 (1977): 1028–34; Robert Forster, "The Achievements of the Annales School," *Journal of Economic History* 38 (1978): 58–76; Jack H. Hexter, "Fernand Braudel and the Monde Braudellien . . . ," *Journal of Modern History* 44 (1972): 480–539; and Traian Stoianovich, *French Historical Method: The Annales Paradigm* (Ithaca: Cornell University Press, 1976); on their use of quantitative methods, see François Furet, "Quantitative History," *Daedalus* 100 (Winter 1972): 151–67; François Furet and Emmanuel Le Roy Ladurie, "L'historien et l'ordinateur: Compte-rendu provisoire d'enquete," *Rapport Collectif presente par le Centre de Recherches Historiques de l'École Pratique des Hautes Études* (Moscow: NAUKA, 1970), and Emmanuel Le Roy Ladurie, *The Territory of the Historian* (Chicago: University of Chicago Press, 1979).

Charles A. Beard attempted to show how differing economic interests influenced the constitutional process and the course of political conflict; and U. B. Phillips drew on the economic theory of capital to explain the course of slavery during the antebellum era. Toward the end of the interwar period and beyond, sociological and anthropological ideas seemed increasingly relevant. Richard Hofstadter showed how pervasive the influence of social Darwinism had become in the thought of the late nineteenth century, while Oscar Handlin explored the opportunities and obstacles to social mobility among immigrants to Boston.[12]

What I mean by "traditional" history, then, is the type of history that was described in the 1954 edition of the *Harvard Guide* and that was practiced during the 1930s, 1940s, and 1950s by its authors and by such other distinguished historians as C. Vann Woodward, Kenneth M. Stampp, Allan Nevins, and Richard Hofstadter in the United States; by R. H. Tawney, G. M. Trevelyan, Herbert Butterfield, J. H. Plumb, and G. R. Elton in Great Britain; and by Marc Bloch, Lucien Febvre, and

---

12. See George Rogers Taylor, ed., *The Turner Thesis Concerning the Role of the Frontier in American History*, rev. ed. (Boston: D. C. Heath, 1956); Richard Hofstadter, *The Progressive Historians: Turner, Beard, Parrington* (New York: Knopf, 1968); Richard Hofstadter, *Social Darwinism in American Thought*, rev. ed. (Boston: Beacon Press, 1955); Lee Benson, *Turner and Beard: American Historical Writing Reconsidered* (Glencoe, Ill.: Free Press, 1960); Robert W. Fogel, "History and Retrospective Econometrics," *History and Theory* 3 (1970): 245–64; and Oscar Handlin, *Boston's Immigrants, 1790–1880: A Study of Acculturation* (Cambridge: Harvard University Press, 1959). On the turn toward sociology and anthropology, see Jacques Le Goff, "Is Politics Still the Backbone of History?" *Daedalus* 100 (Winter 1971): 1–19; Richard Hofstadter, "History and Sociology in the United States," in *Sociology and History: Methods*, ed. Seymour M. Lipset and Richard Hofstadter (New York: Basic Books, 1968); Edward Saveth, ed., *American History and the Social Sciences* (New York: Free Press, 1964); Lawrence Stone, "History and the Social Sciences in the Twentieth Century," in *The Future of History*, ed. Charles F. Delzell (Nashville: Vanderbilt University Press, 1977). Cf. Hughes, *Consciousness and Society*, and Felix Gilbert, "Post Scriptum," *Daedalus* 100 (Spring 1971): 520–30.

Fernand Braudel in France. The traditional historians aspired to portray the entire range of human experience, to capture all of the essential features of the civilizations they were studying, and to do so in a way that would clearly have relevance to the present. They were continually searching for "synthesizing principles" that would allow them to relate in a meaningful way the myriad of facts that they were uncovering. This search led increasingly to generalizations that were emanating from the social sciences. While some found that the economic interpretation of history provided the best "conceptual framework upon which to order the whole," others preferred the sociological or cultural conceptions. But the most common tendency was to be eclectic. Historians increasingly took from each of the social sciences those ideas that could add power and depth to their analyses, without committing themselves to one all-embracing view of human behavior or historical evolution. An intuitive notion of "imaginative understanding" or "historical imagination" remained the basis for overall thematic integration.[13]

Despite the large and increasing role of social-scientific thought in their work, many traditional historians have been wary about the generalizations produced by the social sciences and highly selective in what they have accepted. "Too careful an ear cocked for the pronouncements" of social scientists, G. R. Elton warned, is "liable to produce disconcerting results," partly because "in the social sciences fashions come and go with disconcerting speed." It is not only the poor control of the quality of generalizations that has led Elton and other traditionalists to resist the scientific embrace, but a belief that history is an autonomous discipline with standards of scholarship better suited to the tasks of historians than those de-

13. Hofstadter, "History and Sociology," p. 8.

veloped elsewhere. Much turns on the relative importance of the general and the particular. Elton characterized history as "'ideographic,' that is it particularizes, and not 'nomethetic,' that is, designed to establish general laws." He doubts that the particulars which historians study will ever "become numerous enough for statistical generalizations from them to be valid," and he is convinced that historians must treat "facts and events (and people) . . . as peculiar to themselves and not as undistinguishable statistical units or elements in an equation." While stressing the autonomy of history, Elton and other traditional historians shun exclusiveness. They recognize that historians can learn from the "social scientist's precision, range of questions, and willingness to generalize," and "may often be well advised to count heads." But they are quick to add that such matters "can never be more than a small part of the whole enterprise." While Elton's views may come close to representing the central tendency of traditional historians, the range of their attitudes toward the social sciences is quite wide, and those who have been more radical in methodology, such as Handlin and Braudel, have done much to pave the way for the new brand of "scientific" history.[14]

However willing traditional historians might have been to turn to the social sciences for insights into human behavior, the majority recoiled from the analytical methods of the social sciences. The mathematical modeling and the preoccupation with measurement that were flowering in these disciplines

14. G. R. Elton, *The Practice of History* (Glasgow: Collins, Fontana, 1969), pp. 23, 39, 40, 41, 43, 55. For thoughtful assessments of the role of the social sciences in traditional history, see Richard Hofstadter, "History and the Social Sciences," in *The Varieties of History*, ed. Fritz Stern (New York: Meridian Books, 1956); Handlin, *Harvard Guide*; John Higham, *Writing American History: Essays in Modern Scholarship* (Bloomington: Indiana University Press, 1970), esp. chap. 1; and Oscar Handlin, *Truth in History* (Cambridge: Harvard University Press, Belknap Press, 1979).

were widely viewed as antihistorical, sterile, and threatening to the most intrinsic qualities of history—its literary art, its personal voice, and its concern for the countless subtle qualities that are involved in the notion of individuality. Most traditional historians valued literary art not only for its aesthetic qualities but as an essential ingredient in conveying the experience of the past. They shared Theodore Roosevelt's belief that "unless he writes vividly" the historian "cannot write truthfully; for no amount of dull, painstaking detail will sum up as the whole truth unless the genius is there to paint the truth." Commitment to literary art did not rule out the exploitation of quantitative evidence, and the *Harvard Guide* has an extended discussion of this category of evidence and its uses. But quantitative evidence was generally considered of ancillary importance. Arthur Schlesinger, Jr., probably expressed the predominant view among traditional historians when he said that "almost all important questions are important precisely because they are *not* susceptible to quantitative answers."[15]

The reluctance of traditional historians to embrace statistical evidence was due partly, I believe, to the degree to which they had come to rely on the legal model for the evaluation of evidence. As Hans Zeisel has pointed out, courts have had a "distrust of statistical evidence," especially when offered as "proof of individual, specific events." Judicial distrust is due partly to fear that samples may be poor reflections of the universe they purport to represent and partly to a belief that

15. Hofstadter, "History and Sociology," pp. 11–13; Handlin, *Harvard Guide*, pp. 22–30, 44–49; Theodore Roosevelt, "History as Literature," *American Historical Review* 18 (1913): 486; Arthur Schlesinger, Jr., "The Humanist Looks at Empirical Social Research," *American Sociological Review* 27 (1962): 770. Roosevelt's presidential address to the AHA remains one of the most powerful and insightful statements of the role of literary arts in the writing of history. It is obligatory reading for all who aspire to master the craft, whether they view themselves as "scientific" or traditional historians.

statistical evidence was a form of hearsay evidence whose accuracy could not be tested easily by cross-examination. As a consequence legal doctrine, Zeisel noted, often allows the "testimony of selected witnesses who are far from constituting a representative sample but will refuse admittance of a survey based on a representative sample."[16] The parallel with views held by traditional historians is striking, and this suspicion of modern statistical procedures, as we shall see, constitutes one of the principal objections by the new brand of "scientific" historians to traditional historical methodology.

There are grounds for an argument against classifying scholars as different as Elton and Tawney or Nevins and Handlin into a single category called "traditional historians." Not only is the range of approaches among traditional historians wide, but the gradations in approach are very fine. One could propose a variety of useful ways of breaking the large class into a number of smaller ones. For some purposes, for example, one ought to distinguish between the older type of political historians who tended to be quite suspicious of the social sciences and the "total" historians who found much that was useful in the generalizations of the social sciences. It was not so long ago, after all, that the "total" historians were the heretics and the founders of journals promoting new viewpoints.

A case can also be made for the proposition that similarities in research methods are sometimes stronger between traditional and "scientific" historians than among the members of each group. In their meticulous attention to details, E. A. Wrigley and R. S. Schofield have more in common with F. W. Maitland or Elton than they do with "scientific" historians who specialize in producing models that explore the implications of "stylized"

16. Hans Zeisel, "Statistics as Legal Evidence," *International Encyclopedia of the Social Sciences* (New York: Macmillan, 1968), vol. 15, p. 247.

facts (points accepted as facts for the purpose of argument, even though the empirical support for these points may be quite weak). Wrigley and Schofield work primarily with quantitative data bearing on demographic issues, while legal and political documents and issues are at the center of the work of Maitland and Elton. Despite wide differences in their subject matter and categories of evidence, the particular questions they investigated made attention to details critical for each of these scholars, although it must be added that the methods of verifying the relevant details, and even the conception of "relevant details," are much different in demographic history than they are in traditional legal or political history.

To dwell upon the differences among traditional historians or upon the similarities between "scientific" and traditional historians, no matter how enlightening such emphases might be in other contexts, would be misleading here. The issue at hand is the identification of the characteristics that have made "scientific" historians a distinctive, highly visible, and cohesive group, despite their internal differences. It is also necessary to explain why the mistrust of "scientific" history often unites traditional historians who are divided on other matters. Little progress will be made in unraveling these issues unless it is recognized that historians who identify themselves with a particular mode of research neither totally reject the canons of the other mode nor completely agree on the canons of their own mode.

The New Brand of "Scientific" History

The time has arrived for the introduction of the deuteragonist. The new brand of "scientific" history, which I will call "cliometrics," entered the historical lists during the 1950s. Although cliometricians are sometimes referred to as a "school," the term is somewhat misleading since cliometrics encompasses many different subjects, viewpoints, and methodologies. The common characteristic of cliometricians is that they apply the quantitative methods and behavioral models of the social sciences to the study of history. The cliometric approach was first given systematic development in economic history, but like a contagion it rapidly spread to such diverse fields as population and family history, urban history, parliamentary history, electoral history, and ethnic history.[17]

17. For efforts to move in this direction prior to World War II, see Eli F. Hecksher, "A Plea for Theory in Economic History," *Economic History* 1, Supplement to the *Economic Journal* (Jan. 1929): 525–34; Crane Brinton, *The Jacobins: An Essay in the New History* (New York: Macmillan, 1930); Sir John Clapham, "Economic History as a Discipline," *International Encyclopaedia of the Social Sciences* (New York: Macmillan, 1931), vol. 5, pp. 327–30; and Walt W. Rostow, *British Economy of the Nineteenth Century: Essays* (Oxford: Clarendon Press, 1948). Discussions of the characteristics of cliometrics include Ralph Andreano, ed., *The New Economic History: Recent Papers in Methodology* (New York: Wiley, 1970); William O. Aydelotte, "Quantification in History," *American Historical Review* 71 (1966): 803–25; William O. Aydelotte, *Quantification in History* (Reading, Ma.: Addison-Wesley, 1971); William O. Aydelotte, "Lee Benson's Scientific History: For and Against," *Journal of Interdisciplinary History* 4 (1973): 263–72; William O. Aydelotte et al., *The Dimensions of Quantitative Research in History* (Princeton: Princeton University Press, 1972); Lee Benson, *Toward the Scientific Study of History* (Philadelphia: Lippincott, 1972); Jerome M. Clubb and Allan G. Bogue, "History, Quantification, and the Social Sciences," *American Behavioral Scientist* 21 (1977): 167–86; Alfred H. Conrad and John R. Meyer, *The Economics of Slavery and Other Studies in Econometric History* (Chicago: Aldine Publishing Co., 1969); Jerome M. Clubb, "The 'New' History as Applied Social Science: A Review Essay," *Computers and the Humanities* 9 (1975): 247–51; Jerome M. Clubb and Howard W. Allen, "Computers and Historical Studies," *Journal of American History* 54 (1967): 599–607; Lance E. Davis, "And It Will Never Be Literature: The New Economic History: A Critique," *Explorations in Entrepreneurial History* 6 (Fall 1968): 75–92; Lance E. Davis, "Specification, Quantification and Analysis in Economic History," in *Approaches to American Economic History*, ed. George Rogers Taylor and L. F. Ellsworth (Charlottesville: University Press of Virginia, 1971), pp. 106–20; Charles M. Dollar and Richard J. Jensen, *Historian's Guide to Statistics: Quantitative Analysis and Historical Research* (New York: Holt, Rinehart, and Winston, 1971); Fogel, "History and Retrospective Econometrics"; Robert W. Fogel, "The Limits of Quantitative Methods in History," *American Historical Review* 80 (1975): 329–50; Roderick Floud, *An Introduction*

Cliometricians want the study of history to be based on explicit models of human behavior. They believe that historians

to *Quantitative Methods for Historians* (Princeton: Princeton University Press, 1973); Furet, "Quantitative History"; Furet and Ladurie, "L'historien et l'ordinateur"; Robert E. Gallman, "The Statistical Approach: Fundamental Concepts as Applied to History," in Taylor and Ellsworth, *Approaches to American Economic History*, pp. 63–86; J. D. Gould, "Hypothetical History," *Economic History Review* 22 (1969): 195–207; John Habakkuk, "Economic History and Economic Theory," *Daedalus* 100 (Spring 1971): 305–22; Samuel P. Hays, "New Possibilities for American Political History: The Social Analysis of Political Life," in Lipset and Hofstadter, *Sociology and History: Methods*, pp. 181–227; Jonathan R. T. Hughes, "Fact and Theory in Economic History," *Explorations in Entrepreneurial History*, 2d ser., 3 (1966): 75–100; Richard Jensen, "Quantitative American Studies: The State of the Art," *American Quarterly* 26 (1971): 225–40; J. Kahk and I. D. Koval'chenko, "Methodological Problems of the Application of Mathematical Methods in Historical Research," *Historical Methods* 7 (June 1974): 217–24; J. Morgan Kousser, "The 'New Political History': A Methodological Critique," *Reviews in American History* 4 (March 1976): 1–14; J. Morgan Kousser, "The Agenda for 'Social Science History,' " *Social Science History* 1 (1977): 383–91; J. Morgan Kousser, "Quantitative Social-Scientific History," in *The Past Before Us: Contemporary Historical Writing*, ed. Michael Kammen (Ithaca: Cornell University Press, 1980), pp. 433–56; Eric E. Lampard, "Two Cheers for Quantitative History: An Agnostic Foreword," in *The New Urban History*, ed. Leo F. Schnore (Princeton: Princeton University Press, 1975); David S. Landes and Charles Tilly, *History As Social Science* (Englewood Cliffs: Prentice-Hall, 1971); Val R. Lorwin and Jacob M. Price, eds., *The Dimensions of the Past: Materials, Problems, and Opportunities for Quantitative Work in History* (New Haven: Yale University Press, 1972); Peter D. McClelland, *Causal Explanation and Model Building in History, Economics, and the New Economic History* (Ithaca: Cornell University Press, 1975); Donald N. McCloskey, "The Achievements of the Cliometric School," *Journal of Economic History* 38 (1978): 13–28; Douglass C. North, "Quantitative Research in American Economic History," *American Economic Review* 53 (1963): 128–30; Douglass C. North, "History: Economic History," *International Encyclopedia of the Social Sciences* (New York: Macmillan, 1968), vol. 6, pp. 468–74; Fritz Redlich, "New and Traditional Approaches to Economic History and Their Interdependence," *Journal of Economic History* 25 (1965): 480–95; Morton Rothstein et al., "Quantification and American History: An Assessment," in *The State of American History*, ed. Herbert J. Bass (Chicago: Quadrangle Books, 1970); Don K. Rowney and James Q. Graham, Jr., eds., *Quantitative History* (Homewood, Ill.: Dorsey Press, 1969); Saveth, *American History and the Social Sciences*; D. N. Sprague, "A Quantitative Assessment of the Quantification Revolution," *Canadian Journal of History* 13 (1978): 177–92; Robert P. Swierenga, ed., *Quantification in American History* (New York: Atheneum, 1970); Robert P. Swierenga, "Computers and American History: The Impact of the 'New' do not really have a choice of using or not using behavioral models since all attempts to explain historical behavior—to relate the elemental facts of history to each other—whether called *ideengeschichte*, "historical imagination," or "behavioral modeling," involve some sort of model. The real choice is whether these models will be implicit, vague, incomplete, and internally inconsistent, as cliometricians contend is frequently the case in traditional historical research, or whether the models will be explicit, with all the relevant assumptions clearly stated, and formulated in such a manner as to be subject to rigorous empirical verification.[18] The approach sometimes leads cliometricians to represent historical behavior by mathematical equations and then to seek evidence, usually quantitative, capable of verifying the applicability of these equations or of contradicting them. The behavior that cliometricians have dealt with so far has generally been represented by single equations or by simple simultaneous-equation models with relatively few variables. These equations are usually linear in form or involve linear or other low-order approximations.[19]

Generations," *Journal of American History* 60 (1974): 1045–70; Peter Temin, "In Pursuit of the Exact," *Times Literary Supplement*, July 28, 1966, pp. 652–53; Charles Tilly, ed., *Historical Studies of Changing Fertility* (Princeton: Princeton University Press, 1978); Maris A. Vinovskis, "Recent Trends in American Historical Demography: Some Methodological and Conceptual Considerations," *Annual Review of Sociology* 4 (1978): 603–27; E. A. Wrigley, ed., *Nineteenth-Century Society: Essays in the Use of Qualitative Methods for the Study of Social Data* (Cambridge: Cambridge University Press, 1972).

18. See, for example, Benson, *Toward the Scientific Study*; Allan G. Bogue, "United States: The 'New' Political History," *Journal of Contemporary History* 3 (1968): 5–27; Clubb and Allen, "Computers and Historical Studies"; Davis, "And It Will Never Be"; Robert W. Fogel, "The Specification Problem in Economic History," *Journal of Economic History* 27 (1967): 283–308; Daniel Scott Smith, "The Estimates of Early American Historical Demographers: Two Steps Forward, One Step Back, What Steps in the Future?" *Historical Methods* 12 (1979): 24–38; Jeffrey G. Williamson, *Late Nineteenth-Century American Development: A General Equilibrium History* (Cambridge: Cambridge University Press, 1974).

19. On the role of mathematics in cliometric research, see Jon Elster, *Logic*

Such mathematics might be thought to be too simple to be useful as a characterization of complex human behavior. Nevertheless, actual practice has shown that this simple mathematics is often a powerful instrument in advancing knowledge of the past. First, by making the assumed behavioral relationships explicit, these models lay the basis for a considered discussion of the circumstances under which linear or other lower-order approximations of more complex relationships are adequate or inadequate. Quite often the narratives of traditional historians, when dealing with relationships between variables, implicitly assume the most simple of all functions—strict proportionality between the variables. It has been shown that when this severe restriction is relaxed and a more realistic functional relationship is introduced, the interpretations of some historical events are greatly altered. Much of the work of the cliometricians has been directed to spelling out and formalizing the models implicit in traditional historical narratives and to considering the empirical validity of those models.

---

and Society: Contradictions and Possible Worlds (New York: Wiley, 1978); Fogel, "History and Retrospective Econometrics"; Fogel, "The Limits of Quantitative Methods"; Kahk and Koval'chenko, "Methodological Problems"; Kousser, "The 'New' Political History"; Kousser, "Quantitative Social-Scientific History"; Lampard, "Two Cheers"; McClelland, *Causal Explanation*; I. V. Milov and K. V. Khovostova, "Quantitative Methods Applied by Soviet Historians to Agrarian History," mimeographed (Sweden: International Conference on the Application of Mathematical Methods in Historical Research, June 1973); I. D. Koval'chenko et al., eds., *Mathematical Methods in Historical-Economic and Historical-Cultural Studies* (Moscow: NAUKA, 1977); Sprague, "A Quantitative Assessment." On the relationship between mathematical models and the empirical assessment of counterfactual-conditional statements, see David Braybrooke, Review of *Causal Explanation* by McClelland, *History and Theory* 16 (1977): 337–54; Elster, *Logic and Society*; Stanley L. Engerman, "Counterfactuals and the New Economic History," *Inquiry* 23, no. 2 (June 1980): 157–72; Fogel, "History and Retrospective Econometrics"; Gould, "Hypothetical History"; McClelland, *Causal Explanation*; George G. S. Murphy, "On Counterfactual Propositions," *History and Theory, Beiheft 9* (1969): 14–38; Herbert A. Simon and Nicholas Rescher, "Cause and Counterfactual," *Philosophy of Science* 33 (1966): 323–40.

Second, the mathematical characterization of historical behavior has helped to identify the critical parameters in historical narratives. Because of incompleteness of data, historians frequently have widely different beliefs about the values of the parameters that implicitly or explicitly enter into their analyses. Translating such arguments into mathematical form makes it possible to engage in "sensitivity analysis"—that is, to examine the sensitivity of the conclusions of an argument to alternative estimates of particular parameters. This procedure has eliminated many unnecessary wrangles by demonstrating that the absence of exact information on particular points is at times inconsequential. For quite often a measurement which is logically necessary for a given analysis may be such that any plausible number, even though it may deviate greatly from reality, is permissible and serves to close the logical system on which the analysis is based. Albert Fishlow, for example, employed this device in his reconstruction of the U.S. pattern of interregional trade before the Civil War by guessing at the share of southern imports that were re-exported and then demonstrating that no plausible error in his guess could alter his results by more than a few percentage points.[20] While such techniques do not eliminate all error or banish all needless wrangles, they reduce them by providing criteria that facilitate the identification of error and the resolution of issues.

It is not analysis but description that occupies most of the time of cliometricians. In this respect, cliometricians conform to Ranke's admonition that historians should devote themselves to the task of determining what actually happened. Just as

20. Albert Fishlow, "Antebellum Interregional Trade Reconsidered," *American Economic Review* 54 (May 1964): 352–64, and appendix. Of course, sensitivity analysis often reveals that small changes in estimated parameters may radically alter an interpretation. Cf. Clayne L. Pope, *The Impact of the Ante-Bellum Tariff on Income Distribution* (New York: Arno Press, 1975).

the nineteenth- and early-twentieth-century followers of Ranke scoured the public archives for diplomatic and ministerial documents that would reveal what actually happened in government policy, so cliometricians have been scouring archives anew, this time searching for quantitative evidence bearing on what actually happened in social behavior.

And so we arrive at the crux of the difference between traditional history and cliometrics. Many traditional historians tend to be highly focused on specific individuals, on particular institutions, on particular ideas, and on nonrepetitive occurrences; those who attempt to explain collective phenomena generally make only limited use of explicit behavioral models and usually rely principally on literary evidence. Cliometricians tend to be highly focused on collections of individuals, on categories of institutions, and on repetitive occurrences; their explanations often involve explicit behavioral models and they rely heavily on quantitative evidence. A traditional historian, for example, might want to explain why John Keats died at the time, in the place, and under the particular circumstances that he did. But to a social-scientific historian attempting to explain the course of mortality among the English, the particular circumstances of Keats's death might be less interesting than those circumstances that contribute to an understanding of why deaths due to tuberculosis were so frequent during the first half of the nineteenth century.[21] Of course these approaches

21. The scope of cliometric research in historical demography is indicated in Michael Drake, ed., *Population in Industrialization* (London: Methuen Press, 1969); Richard A. Easterlin, "Population Issues in American Economic History: A Survey and Critique," in *Recent Developments in the Study of Business and Economic History*, ed. Robert E. Gallman, *Research in Economic History*, Supplement 1 (1977): 131–58; Michael W. Flinn, *British Population Growth, 1700–1850* (London: Macmillan, 1970); Michael W. Flinn, *The European Demographic System, 1500–1820* (Baltimore: Johns Hopkins University Press, 1981); Michael W. Flinn et al., *Scottish Population History, From the 17th Century to the 1930s* (Cambridge: Cambridge University Press, 1977); D. V.

are neither mutually exclusive nor in any sense antagonistic, although partisans of the two approaches often behave as if they were.

Some scholars treat quantification as *the* characteristic that identifies cliometricians. Quantification is more commonly encountered in cliometric work than the explicit mathematical modeling of behavior, but it is not a universal characteristic of such work. The term "cliometrician" embraces scholars who, although they rarely use numbers or mathematical notation, nevertheless base their research on explicit social science models. For reasons already suggested, and more fully discussed in the next section of this paper, no single characteristic can be used to distinguish between traditional and "scientific" historians, although a scholar's attitude toward the autonomy of history may go further in that direction than any other particular characteristic. "Scientific" historians generally view history as a field of applied social science, contending that the analytical and statistical methods of these fields are as relevant to the study of the past as they are to contemporary problems. Traditional historians often and vigorously dispute

Glass and D. E. C. Eversley, *Population in History: Essays in Historical Demography* (London: E. Arnold, 1965); Arthur E. Imhof, "The Analysis of Eighteenth-Century Causes of Death: Some Methodological Considerations," *Historical Methods* 11 (1978): 3–35; Arthur E. Imhof, "The Computer in Social History: Historical Demography in Germany," *Computers and the Humanities* 12 (1978): 227–36; Kenneth A. Lockridge, "Historical Demography," in Delzell, *The Future of History*, pp. 53–64; Ronald D. Lee, ed., *Population Patterns in the Past* (New York: Academic Press, 1977); Thomas McKeown, *The Modern Rise of Population* (New York: Academic Press, 1976); Daniel Scott Smith, "A Homeostatic Demographic Regime: Patterns in West European Family Reconstruction Studies," in Lee, *Population Patterns*, pp. 19–51; Tilly, *Historical Studies*; Richard T. Vann, "History and Demography," *History and Theory, Beiheft 9* (1969): 64–78; E. A. Wrigley and R. S. Schofield, *The Population History of England, 1541–1871: A Reconstruction* (London: Edward Arnold, 1981); Vinovskis, "Recent Trends in American Historical Demography."

that judgment. Handlin, J.H. Hexter, and Elton, among others, argue that history is a distinct branch of knowledge which (although it draws on the social and natural sciences, on literature and the other humanities, and on law) has a mode of thought that is quite distinct from those prevailing in other disciplines.[22]

Some scholars believe that the hallmark of cliometrics is the use of social science theories to interpret history. Yet long before the cliometricians appeared on the scene many traditional historians (especially those identified with the movement for "total history") had turned to the social sciences for generalizations that could be used to order their evidence. When Elton criticized certain colleagues for imposing extraneous theories on history, his principal target was not the cliometricians but such traditional historians as Stone and Braudel, who have repeatedly drawn on sociological, anthropological, and economic theories for their synthesizing principles and interpretive frameworks. Cliometricians differ from these social-scientific traditionalists in their manner of employing social science theories rather than in a greater willingness to do so. Social-scientific traditionalists generally use theory, Elton points out, as "a form of analogical argument." For example, "nineteenth century Bantus and Polynesians" have been used to explain "pre-Columbian America and German forest tribes," comparisons so farfetched, according to Elton, that their value, "even their capacity to suggest new questions and insights," is "very problematical."[23] Historians who use social science

22. Handlin, *Truth in History*, esp. chap. 10; J. H. Hexter, "History: The Rhetoric of History," *International Encyclopedia of the Social Sciences* 6 (New York: Macmillan, 1968), pp. 368–94; Elton, *Practice of History*, esp. pp. 20–24, 36–56.
23. Elton, *Practice of History*, pp. 46–47.

theories in this informal way rarely test the applicability of the theories to the particular historical situations on which they are imposed. Many contend that formal tests of theories have no place in history and deny that significant historical questions can be answered by the quantitative tests that are common in cliometric work. The formulation of social science theories in a manner that lends to rigorous testing of their applicability to specific historical circumstances, and the execution of such tests, distinguishes cliometricians from traditional historians.

Methods of authenticating evidence also serve to distinguish the two groups. The methods that traditional historians have developed for authenticating evidence were geared more to specific events involving specific individuals than to repetitive events involving large groups of individuals. Of what use is the criterion that an historian must seek two corroborating opinions, if the point at issue is whether the standard of living of the English working class declined during the Industrial Revolution? There were scores of different opinions on this question and even a fairly unresourceful historian would have no difficulty in discovering two or even several witnesses who shared a particular view. But such a limited degree of accord could also be established for directly opposed views.[24]

Indeed, the very concept of decline in the standard of living is much different for a group than for an individual. Even in the worst depressions, when the economic circumstances of most individuals are deteriorating, there are some individuals whose economic circumstances are improving. Methods of analysis that are appropriate for determining whether George Washington's income declined during the postrevolutionary

24. See Arthur J. Taylor, ed., *The Standard of Living in Britain in the Industrial Revolution* (London: Methuen, 1975) for a survey and assessment of this debate to 1975.

years may not do for the determination of whether or not the income of American slaveowners as a class declined.

Simple transposition of techniques that work quite well for the analysis of individual behavior may do more to distort than to clarify collective behavior. An individual who had so politically split a personality that he simultaneously embraced the policies of a revolutionary party and their most ardent opponents would be classified as psychotic. Yet such split behavior is normal in the case of nations, churches, classes, and other substantial social, political, and economic formations. Whatever the qualities that give individuals a group identity, one never encounters such uniformity in their positions, attitudes, and responses that they can be treated as having an identical personality. Explaining the outcome of parliamentary struggles involving a large number of individuals thus frequently poses problems that are quite different from the explanation of the behavior of an absolute monarch, of a prime minister of a democratic government, or of a few of the leaders in a parliament.

This point is recognized by both traditional and "scientific" historians, and both groups have sought to come to grips with the problems of studying collective behavior in their own ways. In dealing with parliaments, traditional historians have tended to rely on the opinions of individuals who were at the center of parliamentary struggles, and so were in a position to know what was going on, or who, although just observers, were of such keen mind that they were likely to have grasped the essence of the situations. Scientific historians have tended to concentrate on the analysis of roll calls and on quantifiable characteristics of legislators or their constituencies. They have sought statistical methods which are capable of squeezing from such evidence information on the existence of blocs in parliaments and parties, the intensity of adherence to various positions, the underlying factors which give unity to (or threaten to destroy) coalitions, and the mind set of particular legislators or categories of legislators.[25]

The cliometric approach would be of some interest even if it merely confirmed what had already been discovered by traditional historiographic methods. In virtually every field to which it has been applied, however, the cliometric approach has not only yielded substantive findings that are strikingly different from the findings of the older research but has also called attention to important processes that previously had escaped notice.

Take the study of family and household structure that was launched by Peter Laslett and his colleagues in the Cambridge Group for the History of Population and Social Structure in 1965, and which has since stimulated similar research programs in the Scandinavian countries, the Low Countries, Germany, and North America.[26] The first of many surprises to emerge from this work was the discovery of an extraordinary degree of geographic mobility among residents of preindustrial English villages, which led, on average, to a turnover of more than 50 percent in the population of such villages per decade. More far-reaching was the discovery that the so-called nuclear or simple household form of family organization (kin limited to

25. The scope and methods of cliometric research in political history are indicated in William O. Aydelotte, ed., *The History of Parliamentary Behavior* (Princeton: Princeton University Press, 1977); Allan G. Bogue, "Recent Developments in Political History: The Case of the United States," in *The Frontiers of Human Knowledge*, ed. Torgny T. Segenstedt (Atlantic Highlands, N.J.: Humanities Press, 1978); Joel Silbey et al., *The History of American Electoral Behavior* (Princeton: Princeton University Press, 1978); Charles Tilly, ed., *The Formation of National States in Western Europe* (Princeton: Princeton University Press, 1975).

26. Peter Laslett, ed., *Household and Family in Past Time* (Cambridge: Cambridge University Press, 1972); Peter Laslett, *Family Life and Illicit Love in Earlier Generations* (Cambridge: Cambridge University Press, 1977).

parents and children) is not the recent product of highly industrialized society, as previous scholars had suggested, but has been the predominant form of household organization in northwestern Europe and the United States for at least three hundred years.

Laslett and his associates believe that they have discovered a "Western" family pattern that lasted for several centuries and was quite distinct from the complex family and household pattern (presence of kin other than parents and children) that until recent times prevailed in some parts of Eastern Europe. The "Western" pattern was distinguished by the nuclear household form, by a relatively late age of marriage (generally in the late twenties or early thirties for women), by a relatively high proportion (20 to 25 percent) of wives older than husbands, and by the presence, in a relatively high proportion of the ordinary households, of nonkin servants who lived and worked in the household from the time of puberty until the time of marriage. By contrast, East European households, particularly in Russia, appear to have been extended and multigenerational, marriage was at a relatively young age (generally in the late teens or early twenties for women), and there was an almost complete absence of nonkin servants and boarders from ordinary households. These and other findings, although challenged by a number of scholars, have stimulated far-ranging discussions of the possible effects on the development of personality and of such important cultural questions as evolving attitudes toward childhood and other domestic ideals.[27]

27. Other cliometric contributions to the history of the family are discussed in Tamara Haraven, "Family Time and Historical Time," *Daedalus* 106 (Spring 1977): 57–70; Tamara Haraven and Maris Vinovskis, eds., *Family and Population in Nineteenth-Century America* (Princeton: Princeton University Press, 1978); Maris A. Vinovskis, "From Household Size to the Life Course: Some Observations on Recent Trends in Family History," *American Behavioral Scientist* 21 (1977): 263–88; Kenneth W. Wachter et al., *Statistical Studies of Historical Social*

Or take the debate over the economics of the U.S. slave system, which began in the mid-1950s and has continued with great intensity down to the present time. Until the mid-1950s it was widely believed that the slave plantations were unprofitable and inefficient enterprises that were kept in operation by a class prepared to sacrifice its private economic interest and to endure economic stagnation for the South in order to maintain its political and cultural hegemony.

The first critical blow to this thesis was delivered by the now-famous essay of Alfred H. Conrad and John R. Meyer, published in 1958. Marshaling the limited quantitative evidence available at that time on inputs, outputs, and prices and using a standard capital model to estimate the internal rate of return on an investment in slaves, they concluded that rates of return on this form of capital compared favorably with rates on alternative investments. This finding set off a passionate debate that took more than a decade to resolve. Eventually refinements in the original capital model and a considerable expansion of the data base, including the Parker-Gallman sample of over 5,000 southern farms and large samples of slave prices and hire rates from probate and other records, placed the rate of return in the 6 to 10 percent range, thus demonstrating the allocative efficiency of the slave economy. The second blow to the traditional thesis was delivered by Richard A. Easterlin's development of regional income estimates extending back to 1840. Both these estimates and the subsequent refinements in them showed that the South experienced a high rate of growth in per capita income between 1840 and 1860, thus contradicting the view that the antebellum South was economically stagnant.[28]

Structure (New York: Academic Press, 1978); E. A. Wrigley, "Population, Family and Household," in *New Movements in the Study and Teaching of History*, ed. Martin Ballard (Bloomington: Indiana University Press, 1970).

28. The debate over the profitability of slavery is reviewed in Robert W. Fogel and Stanley L. Engerman, *Time on the Cross*, 2 vols. (Boston: Little,

These twin blows to the traditional interpretation shifted
cliometric attention to the question of the relative technical
efficiency of slave and free agriculture in input utilization.
While it is premature to declare this question settled, a consensus
has emerged on one critical point. It is now clear that the
previous view that slave agriculture was less efficient than
free agriculture is incorrect. What remains to be resolved is
the exact margin of the advantage enjoyed by slave plantations
and the explanation for this margin.[29]

The new discoveries and challenges to old interpretations
caught the imagination of younger scholars trained in both
history and the social sciences. The cliometric approach developed most rapidly in economic history and has been the
predominant form of research in this field, at least in the
United States, for over a decade. The majority of the articles
published in the main economic history journals of the United
States are now quite mathematical, and cliometricians predominate in the leadership of the Economic History Association.

Brown, 1974), vol. 1, chap. 3, and vol. 2, pp. 54–87. The debate on antebellum
southern economic growth is reviewed in Robert E. Gallman, "Slavery and
Southern Economic Growth," *Southern Economic Journal* 45 (1979): 1007–
22. Cf. Eugene Genovese and Elizabeth Fox-Genovese, "The Slave Economies
in Political Perspective," *Journal of American History* 66 (1979): 7–23; Harold
D. Woodman, "Economic History and Economic Theory: The New Economic
History in America," *Journal of Interdisciplinary History* 3 (1972): 322–50;
Gavin Wright, *The Political Economy of the Cotton South* (New York: W. W.
Norton, 1978).

29. Contributions to the debate on the efficiency of slave agriculture include
Paul A. David et al., *Reckoning With Slavery* (New York: Oxford University
Press, 1976); Paul A. David and Peter Temin, "Explaining the Relative Efficiency
of Slave Agriculture in the Antebellum South: Comment," *American Economic
Review* 69 (1979): 213–18; Fogel and Engerman, *Time on the Cross*; Robert
W. Fogel and Stanley L. Engerman, "Explaining the Relative Efficiency of
Slave Agriculture in the Antebellum South," *American Economic Review* 67
(1977): 275–96; Robert W. Fogel and Stanely L. Engerman, "Explaining the
Relative Efficiency of Slave Agriculture in the Antebellum South: Reply,"
American Economic Review 70 (Sept. 1980): 672–90; Gavin Wright, "The
Efficiency of Slavery: Another Interpretation," *American Economic Review* 69
(1979): 219–26.

The rapidity of this transformation is due partly to the encouragement given to the new mode of research by the older, more traditional economic historians, who generally welcomed and encouraged the experiments of their younger colleagues.[30] The large library of economic models upon which cliometricians could draw and the relative ease of applying these models to the issues of economic history also contributed to the pace.

Cliometricians working in political, social, and intellectual history faced a more difficult challenge. The problems they sought to master were inherently more difficult than those in economic history, and the library of social science models on which they could draw was more skimpy. They also encountered far more resistance to their efforts among the traditional historians in their fields, and the editors of the mainline U.S. history journals showed little interest in their papers. As a consequence, a number of new journals which catered to the new mode of research came into being and have flourished: among them, *Historical Methods*, the *Journal of Social History*,

30. Assessments of the development of the cliometric approach in economic history include Andreano, *The New Economic History*; Thomas C. Cochran, "Economic History, Old and New," *American Historical Review* 74 (1964): 1561–72; Donald C. Coleman, "The Model Game," *Economic History Review* 30 (1977): 346–51; Stanley L. Engerman, "Recent Developments in American Economic History," *Social Science History* 2 (1977): 72–89; Habakkuk, "Economic History"; R. M. Hartwell, "Is The New Economic History and Export Product? A Comment on J. R. T. Hughes," in *Essays on a Mature Economy*, ed. Donald N. McCloskey (Princeton: Princeton University Press, 1971), pp. 413–22; Jonathan R. T. Hughes, "Is The New Economic History an Export Product?" in McCloskey, *Essays on a Mature Economy*, pp. 401–12; Maurice Levy-Leboyer, "La 'New Economic History,'" *Annales* 24 (1969): 1035–69; Peter Mathias, "Economic History—Direct and Oblique," in Ballard, *New Movements*; McCloskey, "The Achievements of the Cliometric School," pp. 13–28; Douglass C. North, "The New Economic History After Twenty Years," *American Behavioral Scientist* 21 (1977): 187–200; Douglass C. North, "Stature and Performance: The Task of Economic History," *Journal of Economic Literature* 16 (1978): 963–78; William N. Parker, "Economic History: Two Papers on the Development and State of the Art," mimeographed (Chicago: University of Chicago Workshop in Economic History, 1972).

the *Journal of Interdisciplinary History*, and the *Journal of Family History*. The pages of traditional journals have recently become somewhat more open to quantitative studies, and most of the major departments of history in the United States now include on their faculties one or more scholars who work in the new mode.

For many cliometricians the progress of integration has seemed much too slow.[31] A recent survey of eighty-three U.S. history departments by J. Morgan Kousser revealed that 64 percent offered a course in statistical methods to graduate students, but in nearly all cases the level of the course was quite elementary. Only 10 percent of the departments offered courses in social-scientific theory that could teach students the art of applying behavioral models to the study of history even at an elementary level. While such courses might, as Kousser points out, overcome the "math anxiety" that now haunts historians, they do not prepare graduate students to conduct serious research in the cliometric mode.

Many cliometricians want sweeping changes in both the graduate and undergraduate history curriculums. But with a few exceptions (as at Pittsburgh, California Institute of Technology, and Carnegie-Mellon) sweeping changes have been blocked by traditional historians, some of whom believe that anything more than a superficial acquaintance with the social sciences is unnecessary and may be dangerous. As Lawrence Stone recently put it, an historian should come to the social sciences only "as a seeker after a specific idea or piece of information" and that more intense training in social science methods would "make it impossible" for history graduate students "to obtain that broad historical knowledge and wisdom

31. The discussion in this and the next two paragraphs is based largely on Kousser, "Quantitative Social-Scientific History," esp. pp. 448–51.

and that familiarity with the handling of sources which have hitherto been regarded as essential prerequisites for the professional historian."[32]

Impatient with the slow progress of curriculum reform within their departments, U.S. cliometricians have sought to bypass traditional channels by setting up various intensive summer training programs to which they could send their students. One of these has now been going on for fourteen summers at the University of Michigan and another for eleven summers at the Newberry Library in Chicago. The climax of these efforts to accelerate the swing toward cliometrics was the establishment in 1975 of the Social Science History Association (SSHA), which now has about seven hundred members and whose annual conferences bring together several hundred scholars. SSHA also publishes its own journal (*Social Science History*) and attempts to coordinate its activities with those of like-minded scholars abroad.

The Existence of Two Modes of Historical Research

And so what we have in history today are two competing research modes—paradigms, for those who prefer Kuhnian language—which for convenience I have called "traditional history" and "'scientific' history." Each mode has a set of traditions that defines criteria of excellence and a set of problems considered the appropriate subjects of research; each has its own methodology and set of intellectual concepts.[33] I now want to define the two modes of research by counterposing the characteristics that distinguish them more systematically than I have so far. The principal differences may be summarized

32. Stone, "History and the Social Sciences," pp. 18, 37.
33. Cf. Thomas S. Kuhn, *The Structure of Scientific Revolutions*, 2d ed. (Chicago: University of Chicago Press, 1970).

under six headings: subject matter, preferred types of evidence, standards of proof, the role of controversy, attitudes toward collaboration, and communication with the history-reading public.

My effort to describe the attitudes and approaches of traditional and "scientific" historians must be viewed in a statistical light. While I may characterize the approaches of each group on one or another question by what I perceive to be the central tendency of its practitioners, it would be quite erroneous to conceive of all of the practitioners as being located at that point. Even though most cliometricians probably agree that statistical methods are a prime instrument in historical analysis, their assessments range from "indispensable on most issues" to "useful on some issues." Among traditional historians today the range of views on this question extends from "often useful on many issues" to "rarely useful and often harmful," with most probably agreeing that when quantitative methods are used with care and restraint, they are helpful instruments of secondary importance.

Because of the wide range within each group, there are frequent overlaps of views from question to question, and a considerable number of scholars from each group fall into these areas of overlap. Those with a mind to do so could no doubt develop fine arguments over whether scholars such as Richard Hofstadter, Oscar Handlin, Lewis Namier, and Fernand Braudel are best viewed as traditional historians who make considerable use of social science or as "scientific" historians who make considerable use of traditional approaches. It would be quite unproductive to quarrel over where to put those who might easily fit into more than one category. The number of scholars falling into areas of overlap has increased significantly during recent years as a consequence of the gradual interpenetration of the two research modes. How far and how fast the process will proceed remains to be determined, but it has not yet proceeded to the point of obliterating the distinction between "scientific" and traditional history.

The exercise that follows may be viewed as a version of "Twenty Questions." Suppose a visitor walked into a room filled with historians who were unknown to him. Some of the scholars belonged to a group called "scientific," others to a group called "traditional." The visitor could not ask the scholars about their affiliation but could ask questions about their approach to the writing of history. Is it possible to design a set of questions that would give the visitor a high probability of correctly identifying the affiliation of each scholar? Posing the problem in this way implies that certain characteristics are more common among one group of historians than among the other, but that no characteristic of scholarship will identify a member of either group with certainty.

Subject Matter

This may be the most fundamental point of difference. "Scientific" historians tend to focus on collectivities of people and recurring events, while traditional historians tend to focus on particular individuals and particular events. I do not mean to suggest either that "scientific" historians do not study particular events or that traditional historians do not study social and political movements. But when "scientific" historians study the stock market crash of 1929, the decision of the British Parliament to end slavery in its colonies, or the downfall of Louis XVI, they proceed on the assumption that these particular events were the outcome of processes that were governed by functional relationships containing both systematic and stochastic terms. Their manner of approach to particular events is quite similar to that recently employed by the National Transportation Safety Board in its investigation of another particular historical event, the crash of a DC-10 at O'Hare Airport in Chicago. The agency sought to determine, on the basis of a knowledge of laws of aerodynamics, properties of materials, etc., and as precise a knowledge of the facts associated with the event as possible, the most likely explanation for the crash.[34]

Of course traditional historians are also concerned with general forces, and they recognize that these have an impact on human behavior. But they would not accept as an explanation of Louis Napoleon's decision to go to war with Prussia a statement of the form "that under such and such circumstances monarchs are likely to go to war." Even if such a general statement correctly recorded that seven out of ten monarchs would declare war under similar circumstances, it would not explain why *Louis Napoleon* went to war. While a traditional historian would deal with the underlying forces that set the stage for the Franco-Prussian war, he would want to know why Louis Napoleon was more influenced by the hawks than the doves and whether he was fooled by intrigues or convinced by a weighty set of arguments. He would also want to know how important the influence of Napoleon's strong-willed wife was and whether his gout and other ailments had anything to do with his acquiescence.

Another way of making the same point is to say that traditional historians often concentrate on problems in which the influence of the stochastic terms are predominant, while "scientific" historians often concentrate on problems in which the systematic terms are predominant. What is background for one group is the central concern of the other. Some scholars might be inclined to argue over whether the systematic or the

34. Carey B. Joynt and Nicholas Rescher, "The Problem of Uniqueness in History," *History and Theory* 1 (1961): 150–62.

stochastic elements ought to be the principal focus of historical research. The answer will surely vary from case to case and will in part depend on which aspect has been most fully explored by previous scholars.

This difference in orientation helps to explain the impatience that cliometric and traditional historians have with each other's research agendas. Few traditional historians will deny that some information on vital rates is useful, but they are bored by cliometric preoccupation with the temporal patterns of fertility and mortality rates and by the endless debates over the timing of changes in the two series. They doubt that much useful information will come from international comparisons of data on household structure, from correlating changes in the land-to-labor ratio with the rise and decline of feudalism, from tracing collective violence, or from the analysis of parliamentary roll calls. Issues that are at the very top of some cliometric research agendas, such as the decade-long debate over the effect of the frontier on the nature of U.S. technology, do not appear even to have penetrated the consciousness of traditional historians. Nor is there much evidence that issues of such high current concern to traditional historians as preindustrial *mentalité*, the ideology of the abolitionists, or the evolution of religious thought are as yet of professional interest to many cliometricians.

Of course there are questions that have attracted the attention of both traditional and "scientific" historians and in which both groups of scholars have paid more attention to the underlying social, economic, and political forces than to contingent factors or particular personalities. This has certainly been the case when both types of historians have sought to account for the origins of the New South, the changing nature of love and the family in Great Britain, or the decline of feudalism. In such instances it is the other considerations that I listed, particularly preferred types of evidence and standards of proof, that distinguish the two modes of investigation.

Preferred Types of Evidence

Both traditional and "scientific" historians must work with the surviving evidence, usually of a documentary nature, that fate has bequeathed, but there are differences in the types of evidence that are most likely to satisfy them. Traditional historians have exhibited a strong preference for literary (non-quantitative) evidence while "scientific" historians lean strongly toward quantitative evidence. To answer the question, how strong were the bonds of affection that tied members of slave families to each other, a traditional historian might call witnesses such as Harriet Beecher Stowe, whose *Uncle Tom's Cabin* gave testimony to the warmth and affection that suffused slave families. Another traditional historian could counter that equally qualified witnesses, such as Fanny Kemble, testified that the slave system was so ferocious, so destructive in its effects, that it stripped slave families of all "tenderness" and "spiritual grace."[35]

In such cases of conflicting testimony (normal with respect to large groups) most cliometricians prefer information on actual behavior to opinions about that behavior, and they would seek data bearing on the entire distribution of family responses to the slave system. Such information is needed to know which witnesses were describing typical behavior and which were describing aberrant behavior. Cliometricians have thus sought information on the structure of slave households; on the distribution of the length of slave marriages; on the

35. Oscar Handlin, "The Capacity of Quantitative History," *Perspectives in American History* 9 (1975): 7–26, esp. p. 13; Frances A. Kemble, *Journal of a Residence on a Georgian Plantation*, ed. with introduction by John A. Scott (New York: Knopf, 1961), p. 95.

percentage of disrupted slave families that reunited when they were free to do so; and on the distribution of the characteristics of the households in which slaves were raised, as reported in the thousands of narratives of ex-slaves.[36] The traditional historian would discount such evidence because of doubts over the representativeness of the samples; he would wonder whether the memory of aged ex-slaves could be trusted and whether their replies were affected by the race of the interviewer. The "scientific" historian would attempt to devise means of estimating the magnitudes of such possible biases.

Scholars who do not like the outcome of a head count often assert that the count doesn't count because the source is rife with error and hence biased (in the statistical sense). Frequently this assertion is put forward on the basis of the most tenuous evidence, or no evidence at all—sometimes just on the basis of ad hominem arguments; sometimes on a priori contentions that it is reasonable to assume the existence of biases. Attacks on bodies of quantitative evidence should not necessarily be accepted at face value; they require as careful an evaluation as any other allegation. Historians are not always as demanding

36. Stephen C. Crawford, "Quantified Memory: A Study of the WPA and Fisk University Slave Narrative Collections" (Ph.D. diss., University of Chicago, 1980); Barry W. Higman, *Slave Population and Economy in Jamaica* (Cambridge: Cambridge University Press, 1976); Barry W. Higman, "African and Creole Slave Family Patterns in Trinidad," *Journal of Family History* 3 (1978): 163–80; Richard Sutch, "The Breeding of Slaves for Sale and the Westward Expansion of Slavery, 1850–1860," in *Race and Slavery in the Western Hemisphere: Quantitative Studies*, ed. Stanley L. Engerman and Eugene D. Genovese (Princeton: Princeton University Press, 1975), pp. 173–210; Richard Steckel, "The Economics of U.S. Slave and Southern White Fertility" (Ph.D. diss., University of Chicago, 1977); James Trussell and Richard Steckel, "The Age of Slaves at Menarche and Their First Birth," *Journal of Interdisciplinary History* 8 (1978): 477–505; cf. Michael Craton, *Searching for the Invisible Man: Slaves and Plantation Life in Jamaica* (Cambridge: Harvard University Press, 1978); Herbert G. Gutman, *The Black Family in Slavery and Freedom, 1750–1925* (New York: Pantheon Books, 1976).

of those who call for the dismissal of a large body of quantitative evidence, on the ground that it might be defective in one or another respect, as they are of those who offer the evidence.

It is not always appreciated that even proven defects in a given body of evidence do not necessarily deprive it of usefulness. Defects may invalidate the source on one issue but not on another, for one purpose but not for another. If, for example, a given register of vital events is known to be incomplete in its coverage of births because of the omission of those who died soon after birth, it could still be used to establish a lower bound on the birthrate or an upper bound on the average length of the birth interval, and it could still yield an unbiased estimate of the rate of natural increase. Such limited information may be sufficient for many historical issues. There is also the question of the magnitude of the biases. Sometimes it is possible to demonstrate that the defects in a given body of data are too small to have a significant effect on the analytical issues that will be addressed to it. So, before dismissing a large body of evidence it is important to determine the nature of the errors that afflict it. It makes a considerable difference whether the error is random or systematic. A body of quantitative evidence will yield unbiased estimates of the parameters at issue, although it is rife with error, when the error is randomly distributed. Even when the data are afflicted by systematic bias, it may be possible to devise techniques that will yield acceptable estimates of desired parameters. James Trussell and Richard Steckel have shown that it is possible to estimate the age of slave mothers at the birth of their first child with a negligible degree of error, from data known to suffer from substantial underrecording of births, by making use of a statistical technique called the "singulate mean."[37]

37. Trussell and Steckel, "The Age of Slaves at Menarche," pp. 477–505.

The worst of all errors is to assume that either literary evidence by itself or quantitative evidence by itself is sufficient, when they are not. Such self-sufficiency cannot be achieved when the object of study is a broad social movement. Moses Finley is surely right when he says that "all the possible statistics about age of marriage, size of family, rate of illegitimacy, will not add up to a history of the family." That history must deal fully with a series of issues about the quality of family life, such as those that Stone has addressed: the changing roles of husbands, wives, and other kin and of relationships between them; their changing attitudes toward each other; and the effects of family attitudes and roles, first on the culture of families and the fate of its individual members, and ultimately on the society, the economy, and the state. It is also true, however, as Finley has stressed on other occasions, that even the most subtle and imaginative discussions of these issues will collapse if they are not based on a rock of evidence as to what is typical and what is aberrant. Stone's views on the array of issues that he tackles (as Keith Thomas, Christopher Hill, and Alan Macfarlene, among others, have emphasized) are time and again anchored on assumptions as to what was typical and what was not, on assumed trends in household structure and in demographic and economic variables, and on the assumed interrelationships between these variables and such subtle matters as sentiment, commitment, obligation, and emotional texture. Can it be denied that a satisfactory history of the family must have both qualitative and quantitative aspects, and that neglect of either may lead the historian astray?[38]

38. Moses I. Finley, "'Progress' in Historiography," *Daedalus* 106 (Summer 1977): 125–42; Keith Thomas, "The Changing Family," *Times Literary Supplement*, 21 October 1977, pp. 1226–27; Christopher Hill, "Sex, Marriage and the Family in England," *Economic History Review* 31 (1978): 450–63; Alan

Standards of Proof and Verification

The traditional historian's model for proving his case or disproving an opponent's case is the legal model.[39] He seeks to employ witnesses of high moral character and ability and attempts to show that they were in a position to know what happened. He disputes his opponent's witnesses by impugning their character, their objectivity, and their capacity to know. Similar standards are applied to documentary evidence. Documents offered in support of a particular interpretation are scrutinized to evaluate their authenticity, to assess the reliability of the statements they contain or the information they report (both qualitative and quantitative), to establish their provenance, and to determine both their internal consistency and their consistency with external evidence. The historian attempts to show that his documentation is more complete or more reliable than his opponent's, not only by counterposing one document to another, but often by critically reexamining the documents and the interpretations of them advanced by his opponent. In a manner that is quite similar to an attorney's cross-examination, the historian may question the alleged provenance of the proffered documents, the validity of the way in which they have been dated or ordered, and the capacity of the authors of the documents to have known firsthand what is reported in them or, if they did have firsthand knowledge, their capacity to have reported accurately what they saw,

---

Macfarlane, Review of *The Family, Sex and Marriage in England 1500–1800* by Lawrence Stone, *History and Theory* 18 (1979): 103–26.

39. Handlin, *Harvard Guide*, pp. 23–25; cf. Harold J. Berman, "Legal Reasoning," *International Encyclopedia of the Social Sciences* (New York: Macmillan, 1968), vol. 9, pp. 197–204. For an extended treatment of some of the issues raised in this section, see Robert W. Fogel, "Circumstantial Evidence in 'Scientific' and Traditional History," in *Philosophy of History and Contemporary Historiography*, ed. William H. Dray et al. (Ottawa: Ottawa University Press, 1982), pp. 61–112.

heard, or did. Even when the authenticity, reliability, provenance, ordering, and interpretation of a given set of documents
are conceded, the historian's reexamination may reveal that
the conclusions that were drawn from the documents were
not entailed by them and are unlikely to be valid.

Traditional historians also follow the legal tradition of reasoning by analogy, of attempting to show that one situation
is quite analogous to another. Eugene D. Genovese in *Roll,
Jordan, Roll*, for example, finds an analogy between slave
craftsmen and the artisans who sparked the radical movements
in eighteenth-century England, France, and the American North.
This analogy is used to support the conclusion that slave
craftsmen "provided the firmest social basis for a radical political
leadership."[40] Traditional historians also follow legal precedent
by the invocation of authority. When Engerman and I computed
an index of total factor productivity to test the opinions of
authorities who claimed that slave labor was inefficient, some
critics replied that the procedure must have been in error
because it was in disagreement with the opinions of established
authorities.[41]

40. Eugene D. Genovese, *Roll, Jordan, Roll: The World the Slaves Made*
(New York: Pantheon, 1974), p. 394; According to Droysen reasoning by
analogy was intrinsic to all historical understanding. "By being in motion,
as ourselves are within, the world without permits us to understand it under
the analogy of that which is going on in ourselves." Johann Gustav Droysen,
Outline of the Principles of History (Boston: Ginn and Company, 1893), p. 47.

41. See, for example, Thomas L. Haskell, "The True and Tragical History
of 'Time on the Cross,'" *New York Review*, 2 October 1975, pp. 33–38; Harry
N. Scheiber, "Black is Computable," *The American Scholar* 44 (1975): 656–
73; Peter D. McClelland, "Cliometrics Versus Institutional History," *Research
in Economic History* 3 (1978): 369–78. McClelland argued that when our
result clashed with established authority, Engerman and I should have realized
that we were in error. He suggested that the source of the error was the use
of a measure of efficiency derived from a Cobb-Douglas production function.
But, as we have shown (Fogel and Engerman, "Explaining the Relative Efficiency
. . . Reply," pp. 682–89), our result is independent of the form of the production
function. The conclusion that slave farms employing the gang system were

The cliometrician's model for proving his case or disproving an opponent's case is the empirical-scientific model. The strategy is to make explicit the implicit empirical assumptions on which many historical arguments rest and then to search for evidence, usually quantitative, capable of confirming or disconfirming the assumptions. On the question of the profitability of slavery, for example, Conrad and Meyer argued that testimony from planter diaries and similar sources was contradictory and inadequate. They set out to resolve the issue by obtaining representative samples of data on the output and prices of cotton; on the quantities and prices of the land, equipment, and other capital used in production of output; on slave maintenance costs; and on slave death rates. The long debate on their computation of the rate of return turned on such issues as the representativeness of the samples, the completeness of the coverage of outputs and costs, the adequacy of the mortality schedules, and the sensitivity of the computations to alternative methods of setting up the equation to calculate the rate of return.[42]

---

more efficient than small free farms follows merely from an examination of the location of the production points in production space. This conclusion holds with even greater force when we use the alternative measure of efficiency proposed by Wright (in "The Efficiency of Slavery," pp. 219–26).

42. Conrad and Meyer, *The Economics of Slavery*, pp. 43–114; Fogel and Engerman, *Time on the Cross*, vol. 2, pp. 54–87. Conrad and Meyer were not the first to argue that slavery was a profitable investment for slaveholders. Lewis C. Gray (*History of Agriculture in the Southern United States to 1860*, 2 vols. [Washington, D.C.: The Carnegie Institution of Washington, 1933]) and Kenneth M. Stampp (*The Peculiar Institution: Slavery in the Ante-Bellum South* [New York: Vintage Books, 1956]), among others, had strongly argued that view. But while the evidence they marshaled supported their case, it was inadequate to resolve the issue. See Harold D. Woodman, "The Profitability of Slavery: A Historical Perennial," *Journal of Southern History* 29 (1963): 303–25, for an assessment of the status of the debate after the appearance of the Conrad and Meyer paper, but early in the stream of research aimed at evaluating the validity of their approach and findings.

Differences in the types of evidence on which proof rests affect the process of scholarly verification. When proof depends on the reports of observers (in the form of letters, diaries, minutes, newspaper stories, books, etc.) or the interpretation of bills, decrees, judicial proceedings, and similar bureaucratic records, the footnote is the critical element of documentation. It directs the skeptical reader to the location of the materials and allows him to form his own opinion of their relevance and reliability, as well as of the judgment that was exercised by the scholar in interpreting them.

In cliometric research, where large bodies of data are the basis of proof, the role of the footnote is greatly diminished, although it is still used to inform the reader about the kinds of materials used and for other ancillary purposes. The critical information is usually conveyed in tables and charts or in equations, and it is impossible to report in footnotes the thousands or tens of thousands of observations from which these were constructed. Even the procedures followed in the analysis of the data cannot usually be reported in detail in the same study since it frequently involves hundreds or thousands of operations. Consequently, the usual practice of cliometricians is to make their data available to other scholars by reproducing their computer tapes upon request or by putting them on deposit with the Inter-University Consortium for Political and Social Research at the University of Michigan, which maintains an international lending library of computer tapes. The procedures employed in analyzing the data on the tapes are often reported in separate technical papers (and sometimes published long before the publication of the substantive work) or else are described in mimeographed papers and code books or in worksheets, which are available from the investigators on request.

These procedures create no great problem for cliometricians, who are used to requesting computer tapes, format statements, code books, and worksheets when they desire to replicate the analysis of a colleague—sometimes in order to build upon it, sometimes to dispute it. But traditional historians are often appalled by the effort that is required to verify cliometric research. This is what Lawrence Stone said when he contemplated the verification of the graphs in *The Rebellious Century, 1830–1930* by Charles, Louise, and Richard Tilly:[43]

In order to discover the sources and methods that lie behind graphs 5 to 8, on acts of collective violence in France over a century—the collection, coding and analysis of which took countless man-hours of many researchers over almost a decade—the reader is asked to track down descriptions of the methodology spread over no fewer than six different articles (p. 314). Few readers will have the tenacity or curiosity to pursue the subject that far. The great majority will inevitably take the graphs at their face value, without probing any deeper. The major findings of the work stand or fall on the reliability of these graphs, and yet within the book itself there is no provision made for discovering how they were compiled, while the multivariate analyses used for explaining the ups and downs on the graphs are likely to baffle all but the most sophisticated of cliometricians. This is a book which lacks most of the basic scholarly apparatus but which apparently conforms to the best standards of scholarship of which cliometric history is capable. It is the product of a decade of massive research, and yet the reader is left in a state

43. Stone, "History and the Social Sciences," p. 31.

of helpless uneasiness both about the reliability of the data and about the validity of the explanations put forward. It therefore poses in its starkest form the problem of verification in cliometric history.

The Role of Controversy

While traditional history has had its share of controversies, controversy is not normally the mark of a successful study. Success normally turns on how widely and how well a work is received. Although there are notable exceptions, strong attacks, especially if they come from distinguished colleagues, tend to undermine the credibility of a work even if the attack is empirically unwarranted. The traditional historian often comes before his colleagues and the history-reading public as an expert witness who has carefully examined all of the issues, and his book or paper constitutes his expert testimony—his deposition, so to speak. Thus distinguished traditional historians sometimes depart from the monographic pattern of documenting each statement in their study by footnotes, presenting only a bibliography of the sources they examined. An attack on the credibility of the historian qua witness, and many of these attacks are ad hominem, has the same force as an attack on a witness in court. It diminishes his testimony.

Controversy is rife among "scientific" historians, and many traditional historians have interpreted the sharp disagreements as evidence of the failure of social-science methodology, and particularly of quantitative methods, in history. This view reflects a confusion between artistic and scientific processes and brings us back to the significance of the artistic element in traditional history. A painting, a concerto, a novel, and many traditional histories can be the perfect creation of one person during a relatively brief period of intense activity. As with artistic works generally, traditional histories normally have a highly personal quality. Scientific creations, however, usually extend over long periods, approach perfection gradually, and often involve the efforts of a large number of investigators. Such controversies as those over the explanation for the demographic transition in Great Britain, the economics of U.S. slavery, the transition from serfdom to bourgeois agriculture in Russia, the structure of households in Northwestern Europe, social mobility in cities, entrepreneurial failure in Victorian Britain, the decline in fertility in the United States, and the social saving of railroads have demonstrated the great complexity of the analytical issues, the large amounts of data that must be retrieved to resolve them, and the many pitfalls that may be encountered in the analysis of these data. Such problems are resolved through collective effort, one aspect of which is the intense debate over the significance and validity of successive contributions.[44] One should not imagine that scientific con-

44. On the debate over the demographic transition in Great Britain, see Drake, *Population in Industrialization*; Flinn, *British Population Growth*; Lee, *Population Patterns*; McKeown, *The Modern Rise*; Wrigley and Schofield, *The Population History of England*; P. E. Razzell, "An Interpretation of the Modern Rise of Population in Europe—A Critique," *Population Studies* 28 (1974): 5–17. On the debate over economics of U.S. slavery, see the sources cited in notes 28 and 29. On the debate over the structure of households in Europe, see Laslett, *Family Life and Illicit Love*; Wachter, *Statistical Studies*; and the sources cited in these. On the debate over social mobility in the U.S., see Richard S. Alcorn and Peter R. Knights, "Most Uncommon Bostonians: A Critique of Stephan Thernstrom's *The Other Bostonians*," *Historical Methods* 8 (1975): 98–114; Stanley L. Engerman, "Up or Out: Social and Geographic Mobility in the United States," *Journal of Interdisciplinary History* 5 (1975): 469–89; Leo F. Schnore, ed., *The New Urban History* (Princeton: Princeton University Press, 1975); Stephan Thernstrom, *The Other Bostonians: Poverty and Progress in American Metropolis, 1880–1970* (Cambridge: Harvard University Press, 1973); Stephan Thernstrom, "Rejoinder to Alcorn and Knights," *Historical Methods* 8 (1975): 115–20. On the debate over the transition in Russian agriculture, see Daniel Field, "I. D. Koval'chenko, Russkoe krepostnoe krest'ianstvo, v pervoi polovine XIX veka," *Kritika* 5 (1969): 31–45; Jacob Metzer, *Some Economic Aspects of Railroad Development in Tsarist Russia* (New York: Arno Press, 1977); Ivan Dimitrievich Koval'chenko, *Russkoe krepostnoe krest'ianstvo v pervoi polovine XIX veka*. [The Enserfed Peasantry of

troversies are necessarily free of invectives or necessarily lead to full agreement among all parties to it. A "new scientific truth," as Max Planck once remarked, does not necessarily "triumph by convincing its opponents."[45] Perhaps more often than not, it does so by convincing the next generation of specialists, who, because they are not so personally involved, can view the dispute with objectivity.

While traditional historians tend to accept or impeach an historical work on the totality of its interpretation, cliometricians tend to assess each estimating procedure and each result in a large work separately. On important questions several different cliometricians may attempt to replicate a given result. Frequently the interactions between critics and investigators will go through several rounds, with each round refining more precisely the points at issue and calling for more exact computations or more detailed data. That is why the process of verification, which may also be a process of modification, is often so protracted. Cliometricians tend to place a high premium on findings that surprise them, but such findings are likely to

Russia in the First Half of the Nineteenth Century] (Moscow: Izdatel'stvo Moskovskogo universiteta, 1965); Evsey D. Domar and Mark Machina, "On the Profitability of Russian Serfdom," mimeographed (Cambridge, Ma.: MIT Department of Economics Working Paper No. 307, August 1982); and the sources cited in these. On the debate over British entrepreneurial failure, see McCloskey, *Essays on a Mature Economy*. On the debate over the decline of fertility in the U.S., see Allan G. Bogue, "Comment on Paper by Easterlin," *Journal of Economic History* 36 (1976): 76–81; Richard A. Easterlin, "Population Change and Farm Settlement in the Northern United States," *Journal of Economic History* 36 (1976): 45–75; Easterlin, "Population Issues"; J. Potter, "The Growth of Population in America, 1700–1860," in Glass and Eversley, eds., *Population in History*, pp. 631–88; Vinovskis, "Recent Trends in American Historical Demography." On the debate over the social saving of railroads, see Gary R. Hawke, *Railways and Economic Growth in England and Wales 1840–1870* (Oxford: Clarendon Press, 1970); Patrick O'Brien, *The New Economic History of Railroads* (London: Croom Helm, 1977); Robert W. Fogel, "Notes on the Social Saving Controversy," *Journal of Economic History* 39 (1979): 1–54.

45. Cited by Kuhn in *The Structure of Scientific Revolutions*, p. 151.

undergo the most searching criticisms before a consensus on their validity is achieved.

These observations suggest the different roles of controversy in traditional and "scientific" history, but they do not define the difference adequately, and it is unlikely that any brief discussion can do so. Although many of the characteristics that distinguish the two research modes are revealed in their controversies, the manifestations are subtle and complex. One cannot, for example, adequately discuss the impersonal, sometimes arid quality of cliometric debates, which repel so many traditionalists, without setting forth a host of qualifications. It is necessary to call attention not only to such exceptions as the emotional storm over the economics of slavery, but also to deal with the connection between tone and substance. The impersonality of cliometric debates is related to the relatively limited range of the points at issue and to the high proportion of the points that can be resolved, at least in principle, by measurement and other scientific procedures. The well-defined research agendas that emerge from such controversies tend to be focused on technical points which, however remote they may seem to be from the deeply human issues that originally sparked the debates, eventually turn out to involve matters of considerable consequence.

Technical points are also involved in the debates of traditional historians—witness the disagreement between H. R. Trevor-Roper and Stone over the interpretation of forfeiture penalties in the bonds of indebted peers or Elton's work on the endorsements of state papers—but many other categories of issues are present as well.[46] The ideological stance of a work,

---

46. Lawrence Stone, "The Anatomy of Elizabethan Aristocracy," *Economic History Review* 18 (1948): 1–53; Lawrence Stone, "The Elizabethan Aristocracy— A Restatement," *Economic History Review*, 2d ser., 4 (1952): 302–21; H. R. Trevor-Roper, "The Elizabethan Aristocracy: An Anatomy Anatomized," *Eco-*

the quality of mind of its author, and stylistic merit, which loom so large in traditional disputes, seldom enter into cliometric history, just as they seldom enter into science proper. The last point raises still another complicated problem, the influence of external models on the styles of controversy. I have already alluded to the role of the legal model in traditional history, but in so far as the style of controversy is concerned, the influence of literary criticism may be more important. Cliometricians have been heavily influenced by the intellectual style of the physical sciences, although the influence of the rhetorical arts is also evident.

To emphasize the somewhat different roles of controversy in traditional and "scientific" history is not to imply that traditional history is short of novelty. Although novelty is regularly introduced into traditional history through sharp attacks on reigning views (as in Beard's economic interpretation of the U.S. constitution, Elton's rehabilitation of Thomas Cromwell, or Namier's reinterpretation of the nature of British politics during the late eighteenth century), it more often enters through the filling in of blanks in the story of history, and especially in opening up new lines of investigation. As Felix Gilbert has pointed out, "one of the great tasks and achievements of nineteenth-century historical scholarship was to establish the main features of the history of European nations from the ancient world to the eighteenth century and to place the story of their development on a sound and reliable foundation."[47]

In the twentieth century the process of completing the story of history has taken two main directions: the establishment of the main features of the history of non-European countries,

_____

nomic History Review, 2d ser., 3 (1951): 279–98; G. R. Elton, Studies in Tudor and Stuart Politics and Government, 2 vols. (Cambridge: Cambridge University Press, 1974). Cf. Fogel, "Circumstantial Evidence," esp. pp. 78–103.

47. Gilbert, "Post Scriptum," p. 526.

especially those in the underdeveloped regions of the world, and the accurate portrayal of the life and times—the culture— of those ordinary people whose stories were skipped over, or only lightly touched, by the scholars of the nineteenth century. Much novelty now comes from finding ways of revealing the *mentalité* of preindustrial peasants in France, the religious beliefs of English workers or U.S. slaves, the evolution of love and the family in Britain, the changing position of the aged in American society, the rise of literacy in Britain or in France, and the movement of women from the household into the labor force.[48]

The exploitation of "new" evidence is another major source of novelty. By "new" I mean not only recently discovered bodies of evidence but, what in practice has proved to be more important, new attacks on large bodies of long-existing evidence that previously seemed of little relevance or else seemed too massive to be penetrated. Elton's reinterpretation of the politics of the Tudor era, for example, as he has emphasized, turns largely on moving from the information contained in the *Calendar of Letters and Papers of Henry VIII* to the documents

---

48. See, among other studies, Emmanuel Le Roy Ladurie, *The Peasants of Languedoc* (Urbana: University of Illinois Press, 1974); Emmanuel Le Roy Ladurie, *Montaillou: The Promised Land of Error* (New York: G. Braziller, 1978); Edward P. Thompson, *The Making of the English Working Class* (Harmondsworth: Penguin Books, 1968); Genovese, *Roll, Jordan, Roll;* Lawrence W. Levine, *Black Culture and Black Consciousness* (New York: Oxford University Press, 1977); Lawrence Stone, "Literacy and Education in England, 1640–1900," *Past and Present* 42 (1964): 69–139; Lawrence Stone, *The Family, Sex and Marriage in England 1500–1800* (New York: Harper & Row, 1977); David H. Fischer, *Growing Old in America* (New York: Oxford University Press, 1977); François Furet and Jacques Ozouf, eds., *Lire et Ecrire: L'alphabétisation des Français de Calvin à Jules Ferry,* 2 vols. (Paris: Editions de Minuit, 1978); Patric Higonnet, "Reading, Writing, and Revolution," *Times Literary Supplement,* October 13, 1978, p. 1153; W. Elliot Brownlee, "Household Values, Women's Work, and Economic Growth," *Journal of Economic History* 39 (1979): 199–209.

described by that calendar. "The provenance of the documents—
the way in which they came to be produced and deposited—
is one of their most telling aspects, and this is something that,
disastrously, cannot be established from that calendar."[49] It
is in the attack on massive but long-neglected bodies of evidence
that traditional and cliometric historians have perhaps their
greatest affinity. Despite considerable differences in the nature
of the documents that are the focus of each group and in the
methods of extracting information, both groups have displayed
a common ingenuity in coping with the sheer bulk of the
evidence and in making once obscure and irrelevant documents
reveal aspects of history never intended for revelation by those
who originally produced the documents.

Attitudes toward Collaboration

Traditional historians do not usually collaborate, except in
the writing of textbooks, where collaboration is common. There
have been various multivolume series, such as the *History of
American Life*, to which a number of authors each contributed
a volume, or such as the various Cambridge histories, to which
a larger number of scholars each contributed one or more
chapters. But in these cases, each of the volumes or chapters
was the personal product of a particular scholar and not the
collective product of the group. The great classics of traditional
history have all had a highly personal voice. Just as it is
Shakespeare's "Julius Caesar," it is *Gibbon's* "Decline and Fall
of the Roman Empire," and *Prescott's* "History of the Conquest
of Mexico." Traditional historians do not consider a highly
personal voice to be a failing, a departure from objectivity.
Quite the contrary, the quality of the mind and spirit of the
author as it emerges from the pages of his history is a central

49. Elton, *The Practice of History*, p. 91.

element in the assessment of the history. The traditional historian is expected to draw moral lessons, and frequently two studies of the same historical question will differ not so much in the statement of the facts as in their moral stance.

While not all cliometric historians are involved in large-scale, collaborative research, such projects are a hallmark of cliometric work, especially in social history. Collaboration is necessary partly because the scope of the data collection requires many hands and partly because no one scholar can be expected to master all of the technical skills required for such projects. In their study of English population and social structure the Cambridge Group, for example, has had to involve not only programmers, statisticians, and mathematicians, but also demographers, sociologists, anthropologists, economists, physiologists, nutritionists, geneticists, and epidemiologists.[50] The basis for collaboration is usually technical, and the moral

50. Private communication with Peter Laslett, August 1979. Other examples of large cliometric collaborations in Europe include the programs on Scottish demographic history at Edinburgh and Aberdeen, the project on Swedish family history at Uppsala, the Institutes for mathematical studies in history in Moscow and Tallinn, the project on German demographic history at the Free University of Berlin, the maritime history project in England, the anthropological reconstruction of a village in Essex from medieval to modern times, the project on the history of French literacy at the École des Hautes Études en Sciences Sociales in Paris, and the project on the Florentine catasto, also sponsored by the École des Hautes Études. Examples of large cliometric collaborations in North America include the colonial history program of the St. Mary's City Commission in Annapolis, the program on economic factors in the U.S. fertility decline at the University of Pennsylvania, the Philadelphia Social History Project, the European Fertility Project at Princeton University, the Harvard-Brown-Chicago project on medieval Florentine dowries, Programme de recherche en demographie historique in Quebec, the Center for Research on Social Organization at the University of Michigan, the Newberry Family and Community History Center in Chicago, the Mormon Historical Demography Project at the University of Utah, the program on post-Columbian population changes in Mexico and other Latin American regions at the University of California (Berkeley), and the joint Berkeley-Cambridge-Harvard simulations of historical social structures. This listing, it should be added, is far from exhaustive.

viewpoints of the collaborators frequently span the entire ideological spectrum. The products of these intellectual enterprises are frequently multiauthored; one recent paper involved no fewer than ten authors.

Personal voice does not entirely disappear from such works but is quite muted, and many cliometricians treat a marked personal voice as a failing. Since they are concerned with facts and behavioral regularities that can be established objectively, personalized writing, and the moralizing that sometimes attends it, is considered to be entirely out of place. And when the course of research unavoidably touches on moral issues, cliometricians typically strive to treat these with a detachment and coolness that repels many traditional historians. This air of detachment, even when moral issues are not directly involved, arouses the suspicion of some traditional historians who cannot perceive the moral stance of the investigators and who fear that what is offered as objective evidence, is not, and somehow will turn out to be inimical to their ideological positions. Some traditional historians refer to these collaborations as "factories" and to collaborators as "helots."[51] They appear to be unaware of the high degree of intellectual tension that exists among the collaborators in such projects and seem to imagine that, like some German seminars of the nineteenth century, they are composed of a domineering professor and his disciples.

Cliometric collaboration is carried on not just within projects, but across projects as well. In traditional history a scholar working on the policies of the administration of Andrew Jackson would not normally consider the work of an historian of the French revolution relevant to his concerns, except in certain

51. Friction has also been generated by the large grants that have been awarded for cliometric research. See the exchange between Parker and Haskell in the *New York Review*, December 11, 1975, p. 61.

indirect ways.[52] But U.S. demographic historians, for example, follow research on fertility and mortality in other countries with great intensity, partly because such findings are often directly relevant to their work, partly because it is of immediate importance to compare the findings on demographic behavior in a particular region and time with what has been established about such behavior in other places and times, and partly because the analytical techniques devised by one investigator often are directly applicable to the problems of another. The members of the various cliometric groups keep in close touch with each other, exchange papers, meet personally whenever possible, address one another's seminars on work in progress, and hold frequent conferences to assess the state of the art. Research centers that are technically advanced, such as the Cambridge Group, have attracted scholars throughout Europe and America. The visits are sometimes brief (a few days or a few weeks) but, especially in the case of younger scholars, often run on for an entire year. Although limited in their resources, cliometric centers such as the Cambridge Group, the Philadelphia Social History Project, the Newberry Family and Community History Center, the Economic History Workshop at Chicago, and the Institutes for Social, Family, and Economic History at Uppsala welcome these visitors.

Communication with the History-Reading Public

Traditional historians place great emphasis on communicating with a public that is wider than themselves. "Historians," said the authors of the *Harvard Guide*, "are not, of course, the sole creators of tradition," for "orators, poets, politicians, clergymen" and many others also contribute to that end. But

52. As when Genovese finds an analogy between the resistance of slave craftsmen and the revolutionary activities of French and British artisans in the eighteenth century. Cf. p. 50 above.

they believed that "more than any other class of writers or teachers," especially because of "their access to the youthful mind," historians influence "a people's conception of its past." Lawrence Stone goes even further, calling histories "essential elements in creating the high culture of their time" and emphasizing the capacity of "sober apparent truth, as elegantly told by historians," to be "more gripping, more intriguing, and more meaningful" than "artificial romances and novels."[53]

Cliometricians do not generally address this wider public and are frequently disdainful of any in their number who attempt to do so. Some doubt the wisdom of entering into moral and aesthetic realms and do not feel that historians have either the obligation or a special qualification to be the moral guardians of the young. They tend to be disdainful of efforts to reconstruct the "motives and feelings of [particular] long-dead individuals," and some believe that however dramatic and compelling such attempts might be, they are "beyond the reach of empirical inquiry" and are "better left" to the "evocative methods of poets."[54] Many cliometricians want to concentrate on the production of empirically warranted statements about the past that have direct relevance to present-day issues and concerns. Many hope that by studying the past they can discover warranted generalizations about human behavior that have force in the present and will continue to do so in the future. The majority of cliometricians believe that the proper audience for such works are not those who read history for pleasure but those who are capable of assessing and validating the

53. Handlin, *Harvard Guide*, p. 9; Stone, "History and the Social Sciences," pp. 3–4. Gilbert (in his "Post Scriptum") points out that, leaving cliometrics aside, there has been a certain weakening of attention to the general audience for history and an increasing tendency for traditional historians to address each other.

54. Clubb and Bogue, "History, Quantification, and the Social Sciences," p. 180.

fruits of scientific labors—not a broad public, but a narrow group of highly trained specialists.

Relations between "Scientific" and Traditional Historians

Overall, relationships between the adherents of the two traditions can be characterized as those of cultural warfare. There was, of course, bound to be hostility since one would hardly expect those who have woven the fabric of traditional history to be unmoved by cliometric efforts to tear it to shreds. It was not merely that quantification revealed significant errors in the work of traditional historians; antagonism was also flamed by the extremely aggressive stance of the cliometricians and by exaggerated claims. As David Landes recently put it, cliometric criticism was almost entirely devoid of those courtesies and tokens of respect that soften the edge of criticism and "make even gall moderately palatable." Some cliometricians seemed to believe that the whole of traditional historiography was so laced with error as to be almost wholly useless. The message to us, said one traditional historian, was to "Retool, rethink, conform, or be plowed under."[55]

Traditional historians have generally refused to accede to the cliometricians. Some have simply ignored the challenge. Others have called upon cliometricians to temper their language and claims and have sought to incorporate cliometric findings into the stream of traditional historiography. But a more common response has been to counterattack in a variety of ways. One thrust has been to acknowledge that traditional history

55. David S. Landes, "On Avoiding Babel," *Journal of Economic History* 38 (1978): 4; Edward C. Kirkland, Review of *Railroads and American Economic Growth* by Robert W. Fogel, *American Historical Review* 72 (1967): 1494.

is frequently too impressionistic, too imprecise and could be improved by formalization of arguments and more careful measurement, but to deny that cliometric efforts along these lines have significantly advanced knowledge, except perhaps in economic history, which is treated as a special case. Another line has been to attack the results of cliometric work on the grounds that the bodies of evidence utilized by the cliometricians are worthless, their statistical procedures inappropriate or misapplied, and their analyses logically or ideologically flawed. A third line of attack has been to argue that preoccupation with statistics and behavioral models has given cliometricians such extraordinarily simplistic views of human motivations, relationships, personalities, and ethics that they are incapable of sensibly interpreting their own findings. The charge that cliometricians are too innocent to be allowed to treat questions of psychology and culture is neatly interwoven with suggestions that they slyly manipulate their statistical measures to obtain results that advance their hidden ideological positions.[56]

The reluctance to acknowledge that cliometric labors have produced important results leads anticliometric warriors to curious positions. Cliometric results are grudgingly accepted but not acknowledged. Some traditional historians, for example, now report that slavery was "obviously" a profitable investment to slaveholders since the value of their estates clearly increased over time—an obvious fact that somehow was less obvious

56. Cochran, "Economic History"; Charlotte Erickson, "Quantitative History," *American Historical Review* 80 (1975): 351–65; Gutman, *The Black Family*; Handlin, "The Capacity of Quantitative History"; Haskell, "The True and Tragical"; Thomas L. Haskell, "Funds for Clio: Thomas L. Haskell Replies," *New York Review*, December 11, 1975, p. 61; Jack H. Hexter, "Some American Observations," *Journal of Contemporary History* 2 (1967): 5–23; Higham, *Writing American History*; William N. Parker, "Funds for Clio," *New York Review*, December 11, 1975, p. 61; Scheiber, "Black is Computable"; Stone, "History and the Social Sciences"; C. Vann Woodward, "History and the Third Culture," *Journal of Contemporary History* 3 (1968): 23–25.

or less conclusive before the long cliometric debate on profitability culminated in a consensus. Nor is it credible that cliometricians, who are so naive, simplistic, careless, and sloppy, can so often reach results that cause traditional historians to alter their positions. It is also curious that studies which are instantly declared to be *obviously* wrong nevertheless call forth paper after paper aimed at disproving them. Rather than being banished, such works become the explicit or implicit points of reference not only for subsequent cliometric research but for traditional research as well. While such tactics may keep some graduate students away from cliometrics, to others it adds the allure of forbidden fruit. Whatever the net result, the fact remains that cliometric influence has increased steadily, especially among young historians who, with or without the approval of their teachers, are struggling to master scientific methods and the art of applying them to history.

Curious positions and grudging concessions are terms that also apply to antitraditional warriors. The anticipated rout of traditional historians has not materialized and history has not been transformed into a science. Cliometricians have had to acknowledge that there are issues for which traditional methods are better suited than scientific ones. Moreover, successful application of cliometric methods requires a deep and thorough knowledge of historical circumstances. Solid cliometric contributions are generally the product of painstaking searches of archives for primary data, mastery of the secondary literature, and immersion in the public and private documents. Such work is a precondition to the successful application of powerful general methods to specific historical situations. No amount of mathematical wizardry or computer magic can shortcut this process. Efforts to do so have led to embarrassing failures.

Recognition that behavioral models must be place- and time-specific to be useful in historical research differentiates cliometricians from the scientific historians of the late nineteenth century who hoped to discover generalizations that were truly timeless—that would be equally valid for Babylon, for Victorian Britain, and for America in the twenty-first century. Cliometricians have discovered that few generalizations cover such vast stretches of human experience and those that do are so vague as to be of little operational value. Experience has revealed that regularities which can be estimated by cliometric methods, such as demand curves for particular commodities, equations that relate fertility to social and economic variables, or equations that describe political behavior, are not the same for all times and places but differ in varying degrees from time to time or place to place. Far from diminishing historical specificity, cliometric techniques have often shown that processes that seemed continuous over time were actually quite discontinuous, and behavior that seemed similar in two places was actually quite dissimilar. Far from abstracting from detail, cliometrics has led to ever deeper probing into the details of the slave system, family structure, social mobility, ethnic influences on popular voting behavior, and a whole gamut of other issues that have come under cliometric scrutiny.

Even in American economic history, where it is generally agreed that scientific methods have had their greatest impact, cliometric findings do not yet add up to a continuous account of economic development over the last 370 years. The new economic historians have made important, sometimes even far-reaching contributions, but these have been on quite specific points within the traditional account. They may have altered, but they have not replaced, the basic narratives of the growth of agriculture, the rise of manufacturing, the evolution of banking, the spread of trade, and much else that has been traced and documented by traditional methods. Some cliometricians argue that their contributions, though confined to a limited set of points, have placed major parts of the traditional narrative in a new light and have extended the narrative in novel directions. The point, however, is that whether cliometrics opens up new avenues of knowledge, overturns particular elements in the traditional narrative, or merely refines some elements, its contribution is to the elaboration of the narrative. Cliometrics has not made narrative history obsolete.

The genuine differences between "scientific" and traditional historians over subject matter, methods, and style should not obscure their more numerous and more fundamental affinities and complementarities. There is much wisdom in Elton's observation that the basic methodological approaches to history (not the exact details of techniques) "were worked out quite early."[57] Cliometricians who doubt it should turn to book I, part 10, of *Peloponnesian Wars* to see how close Thucydides was to their style (or they to his) when he estimated the size of the assault force on Troy, a point that is critical in establishing his contention that the Peloponnesian wars overshadowed all previous ones in Greek history. Traditional historians and others who doubt the possibility of blending poetics and counting should turn to Lincoln's Cooper Institute address (February 27, 1860) for a magnificent mid-nineteenth-century example of such a blend.

The grudging concessions on both sides are tacit admissions that neither mode of research by itself is adequate to deal with all of the questions that concern historians. To explain the outbreak of the Civil War, for example, one must deal not only with systematic forces in the economic, social, ideological, and political spheres that may have made such a crisis likely, but also with the role of particular personalities, unique events, decisions that could well have gone differently, blunders,

57. Elton, *The Practice of History*, p. 6.

and a host of other contingent factors that loomed large in the actual course of events. Thus, while "scientific" and traditional history are different and, in some respects, competing modes of research, they are neither mutually exclusive nor intrinsically antagonistic. Quite the contrary, precisely because each mode has a comparative advantage in certain domains of research, they supplement and enrich each other. It seems reasonable to believe that as the tendency toward the interpenetration of the two modes continues, the intensity of the cultural conflict between them will diminish. Those who have studied cultural wars know, however, that irrational factors often have as much to do with the course of such conflicts as rational ones. Is it self-delusion to assume that historians are more likely to benefit from the lessons of history than other folk? I cannot free myself of the belief that in this case rationality will prevail.[58]

---

58. I am indebted to Professor Ephim Fogel of Cornell University for the many helpful suggestions regarding the presentation of the material in this essay.

2 TWO KINDS OF HISTORY

G. R. Elton

The issues raised in Professor Fogel's paper bear directly on the claims which history can make for its place in the world of academic disciplines. They must also be debated and resolved if history is to continue its hold on the attention of nonhistorians, interested in the past, concerned to know whether the past can help the present, and bewildered by the disputes among the experts. Some of those issues, it is true—especially those grave matters of internecine warfare and the battles for control of departments—look peculiarly American to me; I cannot find them in England and therefore cannot argue from experience. On others I have written before this at some length, which must excuse relative brevity here.[1] That leaves plenty of important points crying out for discussion.

I must start by stating my agreement with Fogel's fundamental point: the two sorts of historians discussed share far more common ground than they have differences. As we shall see, they are all historians first and practitioners of definable methods second, because they are all concerned with understanding the past. Nor, as Fogel points out, is the desire (nowadays entertained by the "scientific" historians) to use history for the discovery of laws governing human behavior at all new, any more than is the repeated failure to make anything of this understandable but misplaced ambition. It is interesting to learn how old even the current notion is that history can supply laboratory material which will assist social scientists in formulating principles of human behavior—a notion much canvassed by some present-day historians who are worried about the "relevance" or "usefulness" of their labors and particularly dear to those who hope to use history in the alteration

1. *The Practice of History* (Sydney: Sydney University Press, 1967); *Political History: Principles and Practice* (New York: Basic Books, 1969); "The Historian's Social Function," *Transactions of the Royal Historical Society*, 5th series, 27 (1977): 197–211 (hereafter cited as *TRHS*).

of current social arrangements. However, the fact that these debates have a habit of repeating themselves does not lessen their interest or importance.

We must begin by considering whether Fogel's definition of the supposed split in the ranks of historians and the terms he uses to describe the two sides can be accepted. On the first point, he is clearly right: since the cliometricians (those who use the social science methods of model-building out of quantifiable data and analytical reliance on complex mathematical techniques) regard themselves as different from and opposed to historians using other methods, the split exists. I am less happy about the names given to the parties. At times, Fogel seems in danger of reviving that burnt-up chestnut, the debate whether history is a science or an art: it is in aspirations after literary qualities that he seems to discern the chief characteristic of what he calls traditional history, while to the other side he ascribes ambitions to follow the natural sciences in methodology and in moral neutrality. The first are warm (and vague), the second cold (and precise). This would indeed be an inadequate set of guidelines, and in practice the terms employed contain more than this. In his analysis "scientific" historians merit the adjective because they use the methods and experimental attitudes which social science has tried to adapt from natural science, not perhaps because they are innately superior as investigators to traditionalists possibly confined to intuitive and artistic methods. Fogel recognizes that what he calls traditional history constitutes an enormous hold-all within which very many varied kinds of practitioners are somewhat uneasily accommodated. I personally find myself surprised by the company I am made to keep. Did I really practice the kind of history enshrined in that peculiar compilation, the *Harvard Guide to American History* of 1954, and have my methods been the same as those of Trevelyan and

Braudel? I cannot help feeling that Trevelyan and Braudel might be equally astounded by the association. Did Lucien Febvre really share my own objections to social science methods? How would that most formidable of *annalistes* like to sit side by side with a notoriously old-fashioned defender of political history?[2]

I really do think that too many distinctions have been lost sight of and that Fogel's "traditional" history comprehends within itself differences quite as striking as those that divide the mass of historians from the adherents of the latest incarnation of that eternal search for a precise, objective form of study capable of framing laws and predictions out of a knowledge of the past. Still, this latest manifestation is young enough not to have yet suffered the disillusionment that came to its predecessors: it still thinks that it has found a way past the facts of the historian's life—that is to say, past that confusion and lack of certainty which to most of us makes historical evidence suitable only for the analysis of given events and problems, without the chance of discovering "synthesizing principles" capable of ordering all social life and its history in a meaningful way. The history of such ambitions (so well reviewed by Fogel) has its warnings for the cliometricians, but for the present they still seem to think that in this hunt they are on the right track. Since, then, historians may rightly be divided into those who believe that techniques exist which

2. George Macaulay Trevelyan (1876–1962), Regius Professor of Modern History at Cambridge (1927–43), author of many books, of which *English Social History* (1944) reached the widest audience. The last of the "literary" (i.e., not very scholarly) historians to gain academic respect. Fernand Braudel (b. 1902), professor at the Collège de France (1949–72) and author especially of *La Méditerranée et le monde méditerranéen a l'époque de Philippe II* (1949); fierce defender of "structural" history against the traditional and mainly political narrative. Lucien Febvre (1878–1956), acerbic cofounder, in 1929, of the journal *Annales d'histoire économique et sociale*, which championed the kind of history that Braudel endeavored to write.

can defeat the limitations built into historical knowledge by the fact that the past is not here to be studied but must be recovered so far as is possible from the always insufficient and ambiguous traces it has left behind, and those who have come to terms with the disappointment implicit in these limitations, Fogel's two parties are real and can be discussed, provided nobody supposes that "scientific" historians have no traditions and "traditional" historians no science.

Fogel circumscribes the issue when he asserts that "what we have in history today are two competing research modes"—two ways (to quote Hexter)[3] of doing history. It will be best to work through the criteria he has employed, in order to see how far his analysis supports this concept of two radically different kinds of historians.

Differences in Method

Subject Matter

"'Scientific' historians," Fogel writes, "tend to focus on collectivities of people and recurring events, while traditional historians tend to focus on particular individuals and particular events." The weakening phrase "tend to" is employed in order to allow for the fact that both sorts can also show an interest in each other's prime preoccupations, but even so the definition seems to me a little misleading. This comes out in two ways. In the first place, Fogel seems to assume that scientific historians engage themselves in explaining particular events from some kind of statistical law based upon their study of collectivities and so forth, but his example—the outbreak of the Franco-

3. J. H. Hexter, *Doing History* (Bloomington: Indiana University Press, 1971), especially the fifth essay which bears the same title (pp. 135 ff.): a sober and sobering review of the claims of scientific history.

Prussian war of 1870—hardly convinces. It is true, of course, that traditional historians will not regard as adequate or even useful an explanation derived from such a statement as "that under such and such circumstances monarchs are likely to go to war"; but are there any scientific historians who would wish to construct such an explanatory scheme? Is it not rather the case that in their mode of operation the question does not arise: they would not ever attempt to explain the outbreak of that war as a particular event but at best expose general conditions (social or economic) which may be seen as conducing to the possibility of war.

Here, then, the difference in subject matter between the two forms of history, while unquestionably associated with differences in their ways of working, goes deeper than Fogel allows: scientific history slights the major part of what engages traditionalists, namely, the event itself. The main conventional charge against the cliometric method lies just there. It is not that its detractors "are bored by cliometric preoccupation" with this or that pattern of forces. Rather they reject the concept of forces as identifiable agents creating or conditioning historical events. To them this concept seems both unusable and inadequate—unusable in that it provides an artificial, and artificially clear-cut, abstraction from infinite variety (a point underscored by the tendency of cliometricians to disagree about the meaning of their computations), and inadequate because the description of the past as pattern eliminates too many ill-fitting particulars and only very rarely assists the discovery and understanding of additional particular events. You can integrate details in those forces, but you cannot make those forces create detail because they have no existence in the historical reality: they are generalized inferences from observation, used as a kind of shorthand in historical explanation, which at best can become active agents only when reconverted into the agglomerate of detail from which they were first derived.

I agree that traditional historians have quite often "paid more attention to the underlying social, economic, and political forces than to contingent factors or particular personalities," but I would ask how well advised they have been in this fashionable activity. An understanding of the past as a pattern of forces can help to clarify one's understanding of circumstances and influences, but it offers at most a start on the task of understanding the past as event and experience. Fogel's examples show what can happen when an interest in patterns and forces takes control. The several historians who have lately written about the history of the family in large sweeps have often found interesting and sometimes significant detail; but when they endeavored to arrange these details in patterns—seeking, for instance, force fields of family affection altering through time—they have immediately seen their constructs torn to shreds by the introduction of massive additional detail. Critics have had no difficulty in producing real people in shoals, involved in love, marriage, procreation, and the bringing up of children, who quite simply refused to behave in the manner postulated by the pattern-makers.[4] Here the error probably arose from the desire to apply the generalizing concept of forces to a theme exceptionally resistant to it because people do behave very unpredictably in precisely those personal matters.

4. The generalizations imposed on the history of marital and parental affection in Lawrence Stone's *Family, Sex, and Marriage in England, 1500–1800* (London: Weidenfeld & Nicolson, 1977) are not borne out by the behavior of a great many spouses and parents. Cf. the review of the book by Alan Macfarlane in *History and Theory* 18 (1979): 103–26; for a case study which contradicts the book's conclusion (one among a number), cf. Roger Hainsworth, "Fathers and Daughters: Patterns of Marriage and Inheritance among the Later Stuart Gentry," in *Principalities, Powers and Estates: Studies in Medieval and Early Modern Government and Society*, ed. L. O. Frappell (Adelaide: Adelaide University Union Press, 1979), pp. 15–21 (appeared 1980).

More common is the error enshrined in another of Fogel's examples—the case of feudalism and its decline. "Feudalism" is a categorizing concept invented to make discourse easier; it never existed in reality and cannot therefore have risen or declined. Controversies over the dates at which these nonevents are supposed to have occurred are exceptionally futile because there can be no agreement about the concept itself, or at least about which of its alleged characteristics shall be regarded as sufficiently dominant to define the moment when the whole thing declined. For instance: if feudalism is seen primarily as a system of government in which authority is diffused through society, it declined in England from round about 1066 when yet it actually first came in on a definition of feudalism which looks to its military aspects. Only those historians who have fallen victim to the tendency to submerge the individual in the collectivity, or to clothe the abstract in a semblance of concreteness, have been able to speak of such things as the decline of feudalism. Marxist historians, operating their rigorous categories, can debate the date at which bourgeois society replaced its feudal predecessor. Historians not tied by these artificialities may prefer to ask what at this point or that was happening to social relationships with reference to real people who could live long lives without becoming aware that they were supposed to fit themselves into those pigeonholes.

Fogel's mistake here is one to which I shall have occasion to recur: what he calls traditional history is quite often simply bad, or not very good, history. (The amount of not very good history lying around explains and excuses the error.) It is for this reason that he finds traditional historians sufficiently like their scientific colleagues to enable him to speak of their tending to do this or that. Traditional historians really concerned with the reality of the past should, and commonly do, know that a reference to underlying forces should be treated as a tool, not a result—as the beginning of research and explanation, not as the product of research and a substitute for explanation. In a particular investigation the historian may, by detailed research, establish the presence of "underlying forces" in a given complex of events, but he cannot use these results to explain another such complex; at best he may allow his new research to be stimulated by that earlier conclusion and may (if things work out that way) see his new research on the new question confirm the existence of those forces. He will need to take care not to let that stimulus bias him toward that confirmation—a very common event in practice.

The real difference in subject matter between the two forms of enquiry cuts deeper. In effect, traditional historians do not eliminate any question about the past from the agenda, though they will regard some as unanswerable by the evidence and technique at their disposal. They can fall into the arrogant error of erecting hierarchies of importance, to suit temperamental preferences—politics above economics, economics above politics, and so forth. Some elevate the history of structure above that of events and make a holy writ out of their own foibles. Good historians should do no such thing but should look only to the quality of the work produced, no matter what sort of history is being offered. Scientific historians, on the other hand, have found evidence and means for a meaningful study of a good many questions that were traditionally regarded as unanswerable. However, the very nature of their methods compels them to eliminate large areas of enquiry from their agenda and to confine themselves to the production of large-scale analyses and schemes touching certain events only (in effect events within the economic and demographic experience of mankind). Their schemes offer valuable knowledge about underlying structures within the historical process (through time), but they do so by eliminating variety and very seldom offer explanations for any particular occurrence.

Fogel remarks on the lack of interest shown by scientific historians in various cases of ideological development; he wants them to remember that men have minds and ideas. At first sight it is difficult to see how cliometric methods can handle human thought, but Fogel has drawn my attention to the way in which the products of thought—behavior and artifacts— may be quantitatively analyzed to suggest patterns and climates of thought as distributed through large groups. I accept the possibility that scientific history can define a "matrix," a complex of conventions within which individual thought operated, more satisfactorily than can be done by unquantified impressions, but I would register two important reservations. In the first place, what results are statistical abstractions very open to error because they identify thought from products not expressly intended to describe ideas; in the second, the treatment affords no means of entry into the individual mind. Abstraction and quantification lead to overemphasis on common properties in the ideas derived from the products, a bias which will ascribe more weight than they deserve to such things as entrenched convention and dead symbolism while ignoring the often far more interesting and important differences. Ideas and ideologies can afford being ironed out far less than economic activities: doing this to them distorts reality. Cliometric treatment of this area of human experience will create stereotypes rather than true particulars. I am far from denying the inadequacies of traditional historiography when confronted with ideas. Too often has it confined analysis to an artificial selection of data: in the past it has too commonly been content with the un- representative thought of a few outstanding authors, while nowadays, influenced by social anthropology, it makes too much of the alleged workings of illiterate minds. Cliometric analysis should assist in preventing errors arising from studying writings divorced from what one may call a milieu of thought. However, such inadequacies once again represent poor work and are not a necessary aspect of traditional history, and most of these faults can be cured only by better traditional methods— more detailed investigations of a larger range of sources, better awareness of the historical setting. By and large, the practitioners of the scientific methods have rightly recognized their inability to handle the historical treatment of thought and ideas at the specific level which matters, an inability which unfairly can give the impression of a lack of interest or even a presence of contempt.

Since traditional historians are obliged to regard no historical subject matter as outside their purview (though they are entitled to regard some questions and a good many answers as pretty trivial), they would certainly merit blame if they ignored the topics studied by scientific historians. If there indeed exists what Fogel calls an "impatience . . . with each other's research agendas" on the part of these supposedly rival schools of history, one must deplore it. However, the phenomenon does appear to be a specifically American one, not so readily encountered elsewhere. I agree that traditional historians in England are liable to ask where all that investigation of, say, fertility rates will get us, but they do so in a spirit of hope that it will get us somewhere. If they feel impatient, it is not that they despise the themes studied but regret the absence of usable results. They are only too anxious to learn about demographic or economic "movements" from those engaged in studying them. These latter, on the other hand, though at times they can express superior contempt, generally concede that their own area of operations excludes much that nonetheless they find interesting. In the intervals of analyzing their concretized collectivities, they too want to know what this or that human being did or thought.

When I assert that the research interests of scientific historians are more limited than those of the traditional kind and are compelled to be so by their preferred method of enquiry I by no means wish to pass a judgment of value. I should like to think that each will go to heaven his own way, and to the other for answers to the questions properly investigated by either sort. The impatience discerned by Fogel, which is fueled by brashness among the scientists and fuddy-duddiness among the traditionals, is unworthy of the profession. The former will have to accept that their more restricted agenda does not constitute a form of superiority just because it seems to include only "large" questions, the more so because some of the questions and more of the answers have at times strayed into realms of imagination only tenuously connected to the reality of the historical past. The latter must overcome their apprehension, even fear, in the face of results obtained by methods which they are not qualified to judge; they must not allow their sometimes justified doubts about the subjects studied by the scientists to become a general rejection but recognize the value of those searching and widely based enquiries.

Preferred Types of Evidence

Fogel's opening statement on this theme seems to me deficient in two respects. As he sees it, "traditional historians have exhibited a strong preference for literary evidence while 'scientific' historians lean strongly toward quantitative evidence." Surely the methods of scientific history compel its practitioners to do more than lean toward evidence that can be treated mathematically: such evidence forms the principal support for their special form of history. On the other hand, the traditional historian's first principle forces him to consider all the evidence, and among that mass of materials strictly literary evidence ranks very low. Presumably "literary" is meant to include all forms of nonquantifiable documentation, but any doubts about the meaning here assigned to the word are resolved by the example cited. If there are historians of American slavery who would be content to argue about its effect on slave families by citing a novelist and a letter-writer against each other, they would (once again) prove themselves to be bad historians, not traditional ones. One can admittedly find scholars who will write history out of what is essentially second-stage evidence—comments recorded by contemporaries or later observers. The large corpus of work produced by Christopher Hill on puritanism and the civil wars in seventeenth-century England rests in effect on overlooking the difference between evidence for what happened and evidence for what people said was happening. Hill almost always treats the second as though it could do duty for the first.[5] I'd like to think, however, that this method (which is exceptionally open to tendentious selection from the mass—to what Hexter has dubbed "source-mining") need not be regarded as typical of traditional historiography. Indeed, so avid is the concentration of most historians upon the impersonal record that it would be juster to charge them with ignoring the use of past observations and of literature as historical evidence.

Harriet Beecher Stowe and Fanny Kemble, treated as witnesses, conflict, and if they are to be used at all that conflict needs resolving. It is not only cliometricians who would try to judge between them by seeking out whatever other evidence

---

5. Cf. especially *Economic Problems of the Church from Archbishop Whitgift to the Long Parliament* (Oxford: Oxford University Press, 1956), and *Society and Puritanism in Pre-Revolutionary England* (London: Schocken, 1964). In analyzing "The Historical Method of Christopher Hill," J. H. Hexter (*On Historians* [London: Collins, 1979], pp. 227–51) missed this fundamental flaw in work which is indubitably solid and influential.

may exist. I agree with just about everything else that Fogel says in this section of his paper, except that I cannot see why traditional history should be identified with its worse prac- titioners. If there are historians who, confronted with possibly biased evidence, would discount it rather than attempt to assess the degree and direction of the bias, they are just not very good, or even very bad, historians: they allow prejudice, or indolence, or obtuseness to take the place of study. Mrs. Stowe and Miss Kemble may be worth using once they have been properly assessed—once one has properly criticized them as sources by establishing the circumstances and purposes that led to their making particular statements. (I incline to thinking that the problem in question—the effect of slavery upon slaves—will never be solved by reading *Uncle Tom's Cabin*; but that is by the way.) I agree with Fogel in disapproving of critics who attack the author of an uncomfortable inter-pretation rather than grapple with the evidence he brings to bear, but I hope he can turn from such unedifying squabbles, always liable to happen when the historian touches on live social issues, to a dispassionate review of historical practice at its best, not its worst.

I know of no historian worthy of the name who does not appreciate that "even proven defects in a given body of evidence do not necessarily deprive it of usefulness," and if some otherwise respectable people have lapsed into error on this point we may treat them with that spirit of forgiveness which draws strength from the knowledge that they will soon learn better. Indeed, can there really be any such historian—since anyone who rejects a body of evidence on the grounds that it has been proven defective in one way or another would simply have to down pen and cease operations? There is no historical evidence that does not lack perfection—none that is not in-complete, ambiguous, and in some way biased. The well-tried

methods of historical enquiry have been developed for precisely
the purpose of reducing these defects to the lowest possible
point, though, as all those controversies between historians
prove, they can but rarely be eliminated altogether. Some
degree of personal judgment will remain in the assessment,
and I rather think that this applies to cliometrics as well.[6]

When one has tried very hard to allow for all those built-
in deficiencies of the evidence, it is indeed annoying to be
accused of having made no effort to compensate for them.
When, some years ago, I studied the enforcement by Henry
VIII's government of the new political and ecclesiastical order
produced by the early Reformation in England, I had a variety
of historical evidence at my disposal—statutes, proclamations,
circular letters, propaganda treatises, court records, official
and unofficial correspondence.[7] All of it posed various problems
of interpretation and assessment; none could simply be trans-
ferred from the record to the account, as indeed is always
the case. Some problems are readily dealt with; others are
not; the commonest—absence of evidence—can become in-
superable. It is quite easy to allow for the fact that legislation
states intentions rather than performance or for the fact that
government propaganda does not equal a scholarly assessment
of the truth. Court records can mislead terribly unless read
with a full knowledge of their complex technicalities: they
form, as it happens, a striking example for Fogel's wise statement
that one needs to distinguish between "what is typical and
what is aberrant." Using correspondence calls for an understanding of the letter-writers and their relations with one
another, as well as a knowledge of the conventions of the day.

6. Cf. my remarks in *TRHS* 27 (1977): 200.
7. *Policy and Police: The Enforcement of the Reformation in the Age of
Thomas Cromwell* (Cambridge: Cambridge University Press, 1972).

All this can readily be attended to by anyone willing to approach evidence with an open mind and conscious that it needs to be technically criticized before it can be used. However, in this particular case I encountered one obstacle that provided a general bias very hard to eliminate. Just about all the evidence available originated in one way or another with the enforcing agencies; virtually none of it came from the victims of enforcement, even when it recorded their words and deeds. I was very conscious of this difficulty and tried to compensate for it, though of course I do not claim that in that endeavor I succeeded beyond all doubt. If I had been criticized on the grounds that I had allowed the bias of the only sources available to direct my interpretation, I should have argued but would have had to admit the possibility. This, however, was not the path chosen by the only positively hostile critic to deal with the book, who, anxious to discount conclusions which did not suit his views, professed to think that I had deliberately restricted myself to evidence so tainted; he allowed the reader to think that if only I had used additional evidence (of whose existence, it was hinted, I was aware) I should have had to tell a different story.[8] A good example, incidentally, of the ad hominem technique of denigration of which Fogel so justly complains: the example shows that this sort of experience can happen among traditional historians too. The critic in question must in fact have been as aware as other scholars are, or as I am myself, that the additional evidence at which he hinted did not exist. However, since my treatment of the necessarily defective evidence available has persuaded just about every other competent critic that I had established a sense of reasonably objective truth when writing history out of defective materials, I suppose

8. Lawrence Stone, *The Past and the Present* (London: Routledge & Kegan Paul, 1981), pp. 107 ff.

he could not have swept my conclusions aside, as he wished
to do, without resorting to such dubious charges.

Thus the problems of evidence always confront all kinds of
historians who need to grapple with them in a state of full
consciousness. If the problem is that of the scientific historian
attempting to extract conclusions by analyzing incomplete and
biased series of data, he may well, as Fogel says, find a solution
in the application of statistical method. If the problem consists
in assessing the statements of witnesses, he may conceivably
be helped by the discovery of more witnesses. However, the
historian's primary task will always consist in discovering the
circumstances in which his evidence came to be born—
the circumstances, intentions, influences attending the occasion
of its creation. This goes well beyond the notion of assembling
witnesses, for (as I hope to show in a moment) the vast bulk
of historical evidence ill accommodates itself to a concept of
witnesses and a legal model. True, when one wishes to understand so elusive a thing as the feelings and reactions of
men and women to the circumstances and especially the
oppressions which they suffer one will have to rely on what
was said, by the victims as well as the oppressors. Witness
of a sort comes into this. But other historical questions exist—
indeed, they predominate—which are resolved by nonwitness
evidence. To return to an example already cited: when Christopher Hill wished to know people's views on the truths of
religion and their function in society, he was right to resort
to pamphlets and sermons. When, however, he wished to learn
about the economic problems of the Church he was wrong
to confine himself to assertions made in claims and counter-
claims by various observers, involved or not. He should at the
very least have checked that somewhat dubious evidence against
other surviving materials such as financial accounts in which
the realities of incomes and expenditures got recorded quite

independently of any bias in the "witness." (Accounts, of course, also require much technical analysis before they can be used.) When that work was done, it was found that the collapse of ecclesiastical fortunes quite often existed in the minds rather than in the true experiences of those "witnesses."[9]

In short, all historians battle with problematical evidence, and all good historians admit all available evidence to their labors, so far as their strength, endurance, and life span permit. All evidence needs technical analysis, which is where the properly trained skills of the historian come in. Quantified evidence (mostly derived from documents) needs highly sophisticated treatment and receives it from the cliometrician. Unquantifiable documentary, and up to a point literary, evidence, which composes the overwhelming bulk of the traces left behind by the past, requires sophisticated analysis and receives it from the traditional historian. Both kinds should, as Fogel agrees, accept that they labor in the same vineyard and that any form of mutual exclusiveness will spoil the wine.

Proofs and Verification

Here we come to an area of rather more disagreement between my text and my gloss upon it. I naturally accept that the cliometrician's arguments are entitled to rest upon his own standards of proof; though I find myself sympathetic to Lawrence Stone's protest against a method which forces the reader either to accept everything on trust or to check by restarting the work from scratch, I will not question the right of specialists to go their own way, provided they satisfy their

9. Felicity Heal, "Economic Problems of the Clergy," in *Church and Society in England: Henry VIII to James I*, ed. F. Heal and R. O'Day (London: Macmillan, 1977), pp. 99–118; the same, *Of Prelates and Princes: A Study of the Economic and Social Position of the Tudor Episcopate* (Cambridge: Cambridge University Press, 1980).

fellow specialists. I merely note that even scientific historians
at times have difficulty in comprehending a colleague's work
and are liable to claim that his arguments cannot be verified
by his evidence or his treatment of it. But Fogel's description
of the standard of proof thought proper among traditional
historians will not do. In particular, the legal model of which
he speaks is quite the wrong one, and argument from analogy,
which he says may be used by such historians, specifically
goes counter to all good practice. No blame to Fogel: he has
fallen victim to dangerously false guides. Since the question
of proof stands at the heart of all arguments about the nature
and validity of historical scholarship, and since it remains
virtually ignored by the philosophers of history—whether they
be idealists, logical positivists, or nihilist relativists—I think
it desirable to go at some length into the nature of verifiability
and the criteria of proof.

Fogel accepts the precepts offered by the *Harvard Guide to
American History* as correct accounts of traditional methods
among historians, suitable to be contrasted with the scientific
methods introduced by the cliometricians—a brave thing to
do, seeing that the opening words of that mixed and muddled
volume speak of "the development of scientific history," by
which they mean what Fogel has called traditional history.
The book is now almost thirty years old, and much has happened
in thirty years. It may indeed still be of value to students
about to enter upon the particular and limited field of American
history, but its attempts at philosophical instruction tend to
waver between inaccuracy and superficiality.

On the nature of evidence, the *Guide* begins unpromisingly
with a major error: it divides what it calls sources into primary
and secondary, defining the first as "firsthand testimony about
historical events" and the second as "descriptions of the event
derived from and based on primary sources." The first is then

said to be "the view of the eye-witness" and the second that
"of the journalist or scholar who comes along later and tries
to reconstruct the story."[10] Confusion could hardly be more
complete. Those later reconstructions, whoever may have made
them, are not, of course, sources at all for what they tell,
though they may contain evidence and are themselves sources
for a study of (for instance) their authors. On the other hand,
the true sources contain far more than the testimony of witnesses: they are all the deposits of past human action, observed
or not, in all its forms. Fogel calls the method of evidence-
testing offered in the *Harvard Guide* the legal model, and
although its authors do not actually use the term their emphasis
on what they call witnesses, their supposition that one witness
can be rendered convincing simply by the discovery of a corroborating witness, and their calling in aid of a Supreme Court
judge fully justify Fogel's phrase. It must therefore be stated
categorically that real historians, traditional or not, do not
assess their evidence or construct their proofs in the manner
of a court of law.

The basic error (Harvard's error, not Fogel's) lies in the
supposition that historical analysis consists in the interrogation
of witnesses, and this error arises from a very limited notion
of historical evidence. The *Harvard Guide* admits only letters,
memoirs, and newspapers to that category, but even in American history there are surely documents that do not fit so
limited a definition—financial accounts, records of courts,
legislative enactments, city ordinances, census returns, private
conveyances, records of enquiries, and so on, and so on. I
have elsewhere[11] offered what I believe to be a truer classification
of the extant deposits of human experience (action and thought)

10. *Harvard Guide*, p. 22.
11. *Political History*, chap. 3.

by the criterion whether a given piece of evidence was created with an eye to influencing the historian or not, a distinction which has its effect upon methods of evaluation, though I also stressed there that all evaluation of all historical evidence must start from one basic question: how and with what end in mind did this come into existence? It matters whether a letter is written to a friend or an enemy; whether an account of income is prepared by a taxpayer or a tax collector; whether witnesses in a lawsuit are (as they were in the Roman-law system) called by the court or (as they were in the old Common Law) supplied by the parties. None of these and many other problems can be accommodated to the witness model, which should be confined to observations recorded for the explicit use of a third party. The *Guide*'s legal model starts from the question, "is this true or false?", which is indeed the question that a court of law would ask when not asking the more common question, "what is the law here applicable?" For historians the second question, which involves no witnesses, arises in effect all the time; the first is at best one of a whole range of subquestions that the investigator must apply to the matter before him. Very few issues and very few bits of evidence are so simple that all one needs to know about them is whether they tell a truth or a lie. Nor do we examine or cross-examine our evidence as we would deal with a witness, if only because the bulk of our evidence is not provided by people concerned to produce testimony in support of a truth or a falsehood: it is produced by people doing things, not observing them or commenting on them. At best, therefore, the legal model covers only a small part of the traditional historian's area of operations, and even at its best it is a poor representation of what actually goes on when an historian evaluates his evidence and seeks to prove his case.

I will admit that the "legal model" might be said to have a metaphorical or analogical validity—that the analysis of documents can be made to appear similar to the cross-examination of a witness. But the metaphor misleads. The cross-examined witness is asked about his claims to have seen or heard that to which he testifies; the analyzed document is asked questions about its origin, its place in a series, its contents of common form, even perhaps its authenticity (did it exist when it says it did?). With a witness we endeavor to ascertain the reliability of a statement, with a document the meaning of its existence and of its relation to a complex of events, not of observations. I therefore maintain that the superficial and similitudinous attraction of the legal model deceives far more than it assists.

An interesting example of what I have in mind has recently come to notice.[12] On 30 November 1601, Queen Elizabeth I addressed her Parliament in what has become known as her "golden speech"—a splendid and cunning oration designed to captivate a House of Commons which had been put into an ugly protesting mood by the Crown's granting of monopolies to exploiters of the common weal. The speech is best known in the version printed by Sir John Neale, who derived it in the main from the slightly later copy of a contemporary parliamentary diary (British Library, Stowe MS 362) which in 1680 was printed as Hayward Townsend's *Historical Collections*. In some places he altered the text by accepting (for no reasons stated) variant readings from that printed version.[13] This is the familiar shape of the speech, full of famous and memorable

12. I am most grateful to Dr. Katherine Pantzer of the Houghton Library, Harvard University, and to my wife, Sheila Lambert, for telling me this story.
13. J. E. Neale, *Elizabeth I and Her Parliaments, 1584–1601* (London: Jonathan Cape, 1958), pp. 388–93.

phrases. Townsend was a member of the 1601 House of Commons, and his account contains points that support authenticity, such as remarks about the actions and feelings of the audience, rendered in the first person singular. The speech was also printed several times in the 1620s, long before the *Historical Collections* became generally available in print, so that Townsend can have formed the basis of the printing only if (as is possible but by no means certain) his text circulated in manuscript. These "pirated" versions, though recognizably of the same speech, differ in important detail by compression, rearrangement, and in places the addition or omission of words. Worse, a totally different version, barely recognizable as the same speech, has now been found in a unique copy at Harvard: it was printed (this has been established by bibliographical evidence alone, no printer's name appearing on the pamphlet) by the Queen's printer, Richard Barker, is dated 1601 (that is, within at most four months of the occasion, the year beginning on 25 March), and claims to derive from notes taken by an anonymous attendant at the scene. There is later casual evidence that the speech was in fact printed soon after it was delivered. The Queen's own script, which, since she usually drafted her speeches, quite probably existed, has not survived; both Townsend and the anonymous reporter profess to record from memory, not from a written text.

The historian wishes to know what the Queen actually said. He has the evidence of two alleged auditors, which differs wildly. He has noncontemporary evidence, in pirated printings, which loosely supports one witness against the other but may not be independent of him; yet it is the other witness whose "testimony" stands embodied in a near-contemporary print issued from official quarters. What, in this far from uncommon case, is the use of the legal model? Weighing up testimony provides no answer, and instead all sorts of circumstances, of which these supposed witnesses knew nothing, will have to be drawn into the analysis. The matter has genuine significance: if Barker's printing were to turn out to be the better version, Elizabeth's golden speech would have to be degraded to mere lead. And yet his is the earliest record now in existence, usually a point of prime importance in assessing evidence. Much more work is needed to sort out this quite characteristic dilemma, and in the main the work will have to turn on the basic question already emphasized: how and why did these different versions get recorded or get printed? It may then be necessary to introduce circumstantial questions arising, for instance, from better attested speeches of the Queen's.

If the comparison with a court of law misleads, those who rely on analogy for proof mislead worse by, quite simply, using inadmissible methods. Thus Eugene Genovese employs the allegedly dominant role of artisans in the radical movements of eighteenth-century Europe to support his view that slave craftsmen similarly acted as the main support for radical politics in the slave communities: this is the example cited by Fogel. By the use of good (truly apposite) evidence Genovese demonstrated the relative independence and superior status of slave artisans, but the notion that they were therefore radicals promoting emancipation rests solely on this supposed analogy. The analogy is used to suggest a probability which is nowhere supported by evidence.[14] Genovese has thus committed two sins against the proper principles of historical reasoning. The lesser, because in this case marginal, offense lies in the drastic oversimplification of European radical movements (an oversimplification derived rather from Marxist premises than from the facts); the more deadly consists in taking a supposedly

14. Eugene Genovese, *Roll, Jordan, Roll: The World the Slaves Made* (New York: Pantheon, 1974), pp. 392–98.

established aspect of one historical event and applying it to
another event altogether, as though by itself it constituted
proof. The point is that no amount of analogy can prove
anything in history.[15] Reliance on analogy—the belief that
finding similarities in another set of circumstances has any
force as an argument—derives at heart from the desire to set
up universal laws of history: if such laws exist they will manifest
themselves in the production of similar (perhaps identical)
outcomes from similar (perhaps identical) circumstances. If
that were so, analogy would be equal to proof. The circularity
of the argument sticks out a mile: analogies supposedly testify
to the existence of general laws because the existence of general
laws leads to the occurrence of analogously significant events.
Only the believer can work with such tools.

   Analogy has its place in true (traditional) history, but it is
a very minor one. It can prove a stimulus to thought and
enquiry. If something under discussion is similar to another
phenomenon already investigated, one may legitimately *ask*
whether similar consequences occurred in the unknown first
case as in the second. But that is all: such similarities *prove*
nothing. Genovese could justly have pointed to the role of
artisans in European radical movements and asked himself
whether something similar might be discovered in movements
among slaves. The analogy could quite properly have concentrated his mind on the role of craftsmen. But since he looked
no further into the analogous case he adopted and gave signs

---

15. Fogel (in n. 40) cites a characteristically opaque phrase from Droysen
to support the view that traditional historians work by analogy. However,
insofar as Droysen's words mean anything at all, which is not certain, they
seem to say that historians can understand the past because it involves human
beings like themselves. Even this is misleading: it assumes a universal sameness
which needs proving, not assuming, and which I do not believe to be absolutely
true. Nevertheless, I accept that being human gives one a better chance to
understand other humans than being in-, sub-, or superhuman would do.

of allowing the analogy to prejudice his mind so that everything found in the evidence would be interpreted to fit the thesis, he equipped analogy with the power of proof and invalidated his argument.

Let me illustrate this further by a case which might seem to work against me. One commonly encounters the argument that revolutions are made by social groups displaying relative prosperity and recent improvement, and not by the really destitute and desperate. The point is supposed to be proved by the English revolution (the work of the recently enriched gentry), the French revolution (led by the prosperous bourgeoisie), and the Russian revolution (the first stage of which had little to do with working-class initiatives). Three different revolutions which all show one very significant element in their origins: surely we have here a useful analogy and perhaps a law? As a matter of fact, from what I know of the English revolution I am a trifle skeptical about so simplistic a scheme (which ignores the effects of aristocratic politics), and I note that in order to maintain the interpretation at all it is necessary to leave out a great many revolutions led by groups in decline and despair. The supposed "law" might be better rephrased to read, "successful revolutions are made by people possessed of sufficient power, while revolutions led by people too weak to win fail," which would give this law the circular tautology characteristic of all this historical and sociological legislating. But let us, for the sake of the argument, grant that the three examples mentioned do indeed show that revolutions are precipitated by the up-and-coming. This would still not justify a historian studying some fourth revolution from using the likeness found in the first three to prove that the same thing happened in the fourth. Thinking analogously could lead him to ask whether the same thing happened again, but he would then have to investigate and prove his case by the strict canons of historical enquiry, which demand that he should study his topic from the evidence available for it and not in the light of another topic and the evidence available for that.

   Good traditional historians do not employ a legal model of testing witnesses, and they do not argue by analogy. Nor, as I am sure Fogel knows, do they rely on "authority" to make their point; and if the authors of *Time on the Cross* have encountered the argument that their procedures erred because the results conflicted "with the opinions of established authorities" they have been singularly unfortunate and ill-used. Apart from the binding force of his sources the historian knows no authority. If his conclusions differ from those previously accepted, he is not bucking authority but submitting himself to the duty to prove his case from the sources, and he is as free as his predecessors were to argue what he thinks those sources tell him. The fact that for decades, even centuries, the history of the English Parliament was supposed to record a growingly successful resistance to royal autocracy has rightly not been used in the debates which now rage over the reality of that interpretation. When I, among others, comprehensively attacked the views of parliamentary history advanced by Sir John Neale and Wallace Notestein, those anxious to reject revisionist notions certainly did not erect their counterarguments upon some trust in the "authority" of those once dominant scholars but tried to address themselves to the issues.[16]

   A duty to prove his case: but how is the historian, traditional or not, to go about this? What will make one case more convincing than another? According to Fogel, the scientific

---

   16. For recent reviews of this budding controversy, cf. R. Zaller, "The Concept of Opposition in Early Stuart England," *Albion* 12 (1980): 211–34; A. H. Woolrych, "Court, Country and City Revisited," *History* 65 (1980): 236–45; P. Christianson, "Politics and Parliaments in England, 1604–1629," *Canadian Journal of History* 16 (1981): 107–13.

historian seeks out the assumptions underlying his own or his opponent's case and then searches for evidence "capable of confirming or disconfirming the assumptions." This method has often been used by historians of all kinds and is particularly popular among those anxious to introduce hitherto neglected areas of study. Historians of "minorities" (including the majority called women) can start by demonstrating that existing schemes assume without question a history built around the ascendancy of men, of the rich, of Europeans, and can then prove the role played by women, the laboring poor, or the Chinese. The method can indeed lead to successful revision, provided the identification of existing assumptions is followed by a thorough investigation of the evidence, as free from counterassumptions as possible. That is to say, the method usefully reopens questions, but it does not by itself achieve satisfactory answers. And it contains grave dangers because there is some evidence somewhere for just about every interpretation of the past, provided other evidence is ignored. Concentrating on controverting an existing structure through the identification of its assumptions can, and very often does, lead to a concentration on that part of the evidence which is convenient. This happened, for instance, in the building up of the Marxist interpretation of English politics in the seventeenth century: it started from dismissing the "bourgeois" (whig) picture of a national struggle against tyranny and replaced this error by an equally erroneous picture of battles fought for limited class interests, a picture which relied on an even more selective use of evidence than had underpinned the views attacked.

It is probably true that when we deal with quantifiable evidence the method described by Fogel—confirming or denying an existing set of assumptions by seeking the evidence that would prove it—can work because the processes employed by cliometricians tend toward the maximum extraction of evidence and the neutralization of bias. Most problems, however, are not resolved by quantifiable evidence, and for them any approach which formulates assumptions and counterassumptions to be established by a subsequent search for useful evidence is perilous. As I have argued elsewhere,[17] a sounder method attempts to avoid all positive and particular assumptions and patterns until the evidence—and preferably all the available evidence—has been at least surveyed with a mind as open as it can be made to be. This is certainly a difficult, even perhaps an impossible, prescription, but I believe it to be supported by experience, and it remains the ideal to aim for. The difficulties can be reduced if the historian remembers that all recon-structions—his own or his colleagues'—constitute stages in a process of growing understanding and therefore remain for ever open to revision, by himself as much as by anyone else, as more evidence is found, questions are reformulated, and adjacent areas undergo development. Major historical problems do not ever reach final solutions, and this is because a term like verification has virtually no usable meaning in history.[18] The historian does not construct chains of logical proof in which events are irrefutably demonstrated to arise from causes or circumstances alleged, nor does he produce results which can be verified in any convincing sense. His proof lacks com-pelling logic because his subject matter does not consist of individual propositions: the complexity of past life produces a complexity of interpretation which renders that kind of proof inapposite. And though all historical accounts can seemingly

17. Especially *Practice of History*, pp. 58–73.
18. While I hold this to be true for any serious historical problem, I would not deny the possibility that some isolated events—many of the details studied in analyzing the problem—can be settled by a process akin to verification. Such things as dates, the presence or absence of a person, or the original language of a document can be established by processes of proof which will yield the same results when applied by another student.

be verified by, as it were, repeating the experiment (retracing the amalgam of evidence and reasoning upon which they rest) the operation does not really equal verification or falsification. It does not amount to verification because historical accounts of complex events must be tested against all the evidence, not only that alleged by the first experimenter: and it does not amount to falsification because historical accounts can turn out to be convincing even though they have failed to allow for all the available evidence.

It would help in all these debates if people could accept that the only "model" for explaining historical method is that of the historian himself: he is not a philosopher or a scientist or an imaginative artist but simply an historian working by the rules and standards of his own craft. For two very simple reasons the truth which he professes to present cannot ever be more than an approximation: it lies in the past and therefore cannot itself be brought before one's eyes, and it is so complex that to put it, or any part of it, on paper distorts by omission, by emphasis, and by the fact that in speech and writing one word follows upon another whereas in the life described the occurrences thus strung out frequently happen simultaneously. History therefore aims at explanations which approximate to an unverifiable truth and are themselves subject to the continuous change which is the one indisputable fact about history. Historical explanations themselves form a part of the history told. The standards of acceptable proof in history thus are the standards of acceptable probability controlled by expert knowledge of the evidence, and the historical account is in itself the nearest thing to a proof that the historian can obtain or proffer. He convinces insofar as he persuades others capable of judging that he has worked honestly and that the story he tells makes sense in the light of the sources available illumined by a cautious understanding of people and their probabilities.

If he can persuade his critics that he has endeavored to search with a minimum of preconditioning assumptions, has allowed his evidence to guide his questions rather than the other way round, has tried to seek out all the relevant evidence, has really analyzed the meaning of that evidence by placing it in context and grasping how it came into existence, and has grounded the detail of his account on source evidence that can be checked by others, he will have produced a construct which carries conviction. Not, however, final conviction for ever: there are no eternal verities in history, which is not to say (a point surely not worth discoursing upon again) that one man's opinion is as good as another's.

This may strike practitioners of other arts as unsatisfactory and indeed tends not to satisfy those historians who hunt the chimaera of scientific certainty or wish to use history for the creation of a science of human behavior and experience. That is to say, it does not satisfy those who should not be historians because they cannot accept the attraction of a study which so often opens out afresh just as it seems to have reached completion. The intellectual and social virtue of history lies precisely in its skeptical denial of the scientific straitjackets that others want to place upon human behavior and experience.[19] Nevertheless, as the continuous disputes among historians show, that approximation rather than certainty is the truth about historical truth: while by no means relative, it is distinctly incomplete and for ever subject to modification by improved knowledge.[20] This seems to me to apply quite as

19. Cf. my remarks in *TRHS* (1977): 206–11.
20. E. H. Carr's famous (notorious?) *What is History?* (Harmondsworth: Penguin Books, 1961) attempted to establish the nihilist, not to say frivolous, view that all historical reconstructions are only each historian's opinions, with no absolute standards to decide between them. While my view, which emphasizes the lack of final truth in history, might be supposed to agree with this, it is actually the exact opposite. I allot to each historian a role in

much to "scientific" history, whose results show no sign of being scientifically compelling to others, as to traditional history. Good history of any kind presents constructs of persuasive probability, held together by the unverifiable proof of evidence properly and exhaustively investigated; and since not even quantitative and quantifiable evidence is ever complete not even cliometrics can produce strictly verifiable proofs in the manner of mathematics or logic. Speaking as an historian, I can only cry "hosanna" to that conclusion.

Controversy and Collaboration

I shall take Fogel's next two distinguishing criteria together because what he says about them seems to me very specifically derived from his American experience, on which it would be presumptuous for me to comment. Having frequently been involved in controversy and very marginally involved in collaboration, I find some of his description rather baffling. Is it really the case that traditional historians tend to be judged by the reaction of "distinguished colleagues"? Who sets up as a distinguished colleague? We are back with the distressing notion of "authority." I cannot think of a case within my experience when an innovating piece of historical writing lost credence under attack from some well-known scholar even though the attack was "empirically unwarranted." If this sort of thing really occurs, it once again reveals the flaws of bad practice, not a characteristic feature of some form of history. Of course, the historian who regards himself as an expert witness may well react with affront to a demonstration that his expertise has its gaps; he may come to think that criticism

---

cooperatively advancing the improvement of real knowledge, whereas Carr leaves every historian encapsuled in his egocentric perfection and equally entitled to rest content with his version. My truth is only asymptotically attainable; his nonexistent.

is directed at his person, not his argument. If he realizes, as most of those known to me do, that he is a member of a group all equally concerned to understand the truth of the past and all equally open to criticism based on the analysis of the evidence adduced, he may still not like being criticized but will be concerned to argue his case rather than assume that he is the victim of personal hostility on the part of a "distinguished colleague." By the same token, those marshaling their critique will, if they realize the truth, direct themselves to the subject matter, not the man. But perhaps they order these things differently in America.

What Fogel says about the role of controversy in scientific history seems to be very much what I regard as its proper role in all forms of historical study. Controversy forms the sharpest manifestation of the normal dialectic of historical research—of that exchange of answers to questions by which we progress to a new and more complete understanding of problems. It is justified only if it leads to a sizable amount of ultimate agreement; historical problems being what they are, only a dreamer would look for total consensus. Thus controversy testifies to the presence of life, to the historian's necessary willingness to listen as well as to talk, and to the unending process of learning in which even the most distinguished "authority" should remain for ever involved. True controversy—the argument over issues and problems—is as much a sign of health as false controversies—attacks ad hominem and ex cathedra—are signs of mental decay. Both occur in both scientific and traditional history, though fortunately the right kind is notably more common than the wrong. At least I hope so.

Total absence of controversy signifies a species of intellectual death inasmuch as it defines an area of operations as deserted and abandoned. For myself, I find even noisy controversies or

attacks from supposedly distinguished colleagues less disquieting
than an overready acceptance of new interpretations that have
not gone through the tests of purifying argument. Such adoration
of fashion seems also to have occurred in both kinds of history.
Nowadays (unless I am very much mistaken) major new theses
tend to go through a cycle in which premature and sometimes
quite prolonged acceptance is followed by overheated rejection,
before in due course the valuable residue, sometimes small
but often close to total, can be identified. Immediate argument
and controversy might well be preferable, as offering a speedier
and less noisy chance of proper assessment. This perhaps
surprising phenomenon arises from the accidents of teaching
rather than research: to prove their alertness, teachers and
students are liable to seek out the latest statements and forget
predecessors. This, I think, happened to the early products of
cliometric research (for example, the study of the railroads
in nineteenth-century America) quite as much as to the "Tudor
revolution in government," to cite a not improper example in
traditional history. Truth to tell, those of us possessed of a
fluent and frequent pen probably get too ready a hearing—
and I speak as one so equipped and so listened to. The reverse
of that medal carries the avenging furies—those who want
to demolish a thesis just because it has gained credence, perhaps
too readily.[21]

---

21. My thesis of a revolution in Tudor government was subjected to examination by controversy in 1963–65, ten years after the book's appearance,
in an exchange among G. L. Harriss, P. H. Williams, J. P. Cooper, and myself
(*Past and Present* 25 [1963]: 3–58; 26 [1964]: 26–49; 31 [1965]: 87–96; 32
[1965]: 103–09). I am, of course, prejudiced, but I would maintain that the
debate proved beneficial, certainly to me: it helped me to a better definition
of my position, the shedding of false components in the thesis, and the
attainment of a point from which it was possible to advance further, in place
of that feeling of conclusiveness which, being young and raw, I had entertained
before being attacked.

As for collaboration (a lesser issue in this discussion), I fully agree that here the two kinds of history manifestly differ. Collecting and "processing" the vast array of detail upon which cliometricians exercise their science does call for the services of groups working together, and this again requires that all involved should work to a common scheme by common methods. There *is* something essentially individualistic about the traditional historian's encounter with his sources: he devises his own tricks for the handling of evidence, the formulation of questions, and the application of analytical techniques. Though cooperation can occur it is bound to be rare and is likely to take the form of working side by side rather than one with another. However, I do wonder whether this individualism goes so deep as to give to the outcome a character overwhelmingly marked by individual moral attitudes. The authors whom Fogel cites are the great men of the preprofessional age for whom the writing of history certainly meant the expression of a personal testimony. We are today no longer Gibbons and Prescotts, and I find it impossible to regret the change. Yes, personality matters and will inform the historian's work, but not to the point where differences in moral stance predominate over the empirical and dispassionate assessment of the evidence. Not, at least, in good traditional history whose practitioners try to strike a decent balance between overinvolvement and total withdrawal. It cannot be emphasized too often that in *good* traditional history, as in *good* scientific history, the quality of the work on the sources alone decides the quality and the acceptability of the history written.

In Fogel's remarks about the rejection by conventional historians of unconventional enterprises I recognize some of my own unregenerate attitudes. Having got to know a little about those factories (especially Fogel's company of brethren and

the Cambridge group of population historians) I offer unreserved
apologies. It is still not the way that I could or would wish
to work, but I have come to respect the willingness of others
to go about their tasks in that collaborative way. As Fogel
says, their questions leave them no choice; and as he says,
individuals inside the group remain very much individual historians with minds and responsibilities of their own. As he
does not say, this is mainly because people like himself make
very sure that collaboration under their aegis in no way re-
sembles helotry.

Communication

I agree pretty wholeheartedly here: one true difference between Fogel's two categories lies in the concern they show to
attract attention outside their ranks. It is hard for the more
traditional historian to accept the guild mentality of his cliometric colleague, even if he does not go so far as the authors
cited who, a trifle complacently, speak of creators of tradition
and makers of high culture. Most historians are content with
more modest publics and results. But they do like being read,
and few things perhaps call forth more readily the nastier
side of respectable practitioners than the popularity of writers
whose scholarship they despise. Again, I admit myself guilty
of such feelings toward, for instance, the soothing pap lavishly
doled out by G. M. Trevelyan and eagerly swallowed by a
large public; and other names come readily to mind. (Note,
please, that profitability is *not* the issue, nor does envy describe
what one feels; rather one resents the success of what are
offenses against moral and intellectual standards.) Of course,
as Fogel says, cliometricians also wish to instruct and edify,
and unlike traditional historians they really seem to think that
they can provide objective guidelines to those who have to

lead the nations. For the present, at any rate, they preserve that mandarin attitude which sad experience has caused to wither among traditional historians.

For the odd thing is that those postures of elitism and contempt for the generality afflicted traditional historians in the days when they thought that they were new, and indeed scientific. Some fifty years ago, the ability to write decent prose could among his peers count against an historian. Then those who thought it science to study documentary sources by strict methods also reckoned that only their likes could assess and therefore should understand their work, and they also held that to write in such a way as to give pleasure to the reader was to betray the proper standards of research. After all, if there are few who can really judge work based on the mathematical techniques of quantification and the application of economic theory, there are not all that many who can assess an analysis of Anglo-Saxon writs or debates over the writings of medieval schoolmen. Why the truth—technical skills are the possession of experts—should lead to the false conclusion that there is no point in talking to anyone other than fellow-experts is not really clear. The error perhaps arises from two weaknesses: a certain lack of self-confidence which takes refuge in esoteric seclusion and an innate puritanism which despises art as hypocrisy. It is a repetitive thing: every new generation of historians who think they have found a way of turning their uncertain, contingent, and inconclusive enterprise into a science with, ideally, powers of prediction, begins by building fences around their "in-group" and by denying that substance has anything to do with form. Time tends to cure these ills.

Let me sum up this discussion of the criteria advanced by Fogel to define the differences between scientific and traditional history. Some are real, but arise straightforwardly out of the techniques employed in solving different historical problems; they therefore do not deny the essential oneness of the study of the past. Some are ephemeral, being the by-products of novelty. Most, however, do not in fact exist except where traditional history is practiced badly, as of course it can and will be. On such matters as the proper area of enquiry (the past in all its aspects), standards of empirical proof, the instructed analysis of evidence, and the function of argument (controversy) among scholars, good traditional and good scientific historians are at one. Only poor work by either sort produces apparently categorical differences; and only consciousness of poor work on one's own part leads to that embattled exclusiveness which causes traditional historians to regard their scientific brethren as uncivilized yahoos and causes the latter to repay the compliment with charges of obscurantist indifference to what really matters. Maitland's seamless garment of history clothes us all.[22]

History and the Social Sciences

We are all historians, differing only in what questions interest us and what methods we find useful in answering them. This fact, however, does not force us to accept each other's methods as satisfactory without testing them and especially without looking at the results obtained. The scientific historians deny the value of studies which do not concern themselves with the great underlying developments in human society and regard traditional preoccupation with particular events as footling. (Braudel, therefore, is an antitraditional historian who happened

22. Frederic William Maitland (1850–1906), Downing Professor of the Laws of England at Cambridge from 1899: the outstanding English legal historian, who combined superb scholarly skill with a charming wit and a quite exceptionally sweet temperament.

to come too soon to employ econometric techniques and refined social science models in the victory of *structure* over *événement*.) Whatever case there may be for such disapproval I will leave to the cliometricians to make; I will look instead at what effect they have had on the more traditional themes which their example has drawn within the outer ring of the magic circle. As Fogel so rightly says, cliometrics, starting from a base in economic history, has been colonizing the history of population, of towns, of parliaments and electorates, and so forth. Of these, I am most familiar with the history of the English Parliament, which may serve as a testing ground.

The methods of the social sciences have so far invaded this history three times, tackling different aspects of it. First came the study of elected members—the comprehensive analysis of their characteristics as people and as members of social groups. The most extensive product of this ambition will in the end be the volumes on members of the House of Commons published by the History of Parliament Trust in London, but since that series is not yet complete, and since it also appears that the enterprise will supply raw material rather than history, I shall leave it out of consideration here. The method—called prosopography by ancient historians, and by Sir John Neale[23] the biographical approach to history—borrowed from the social sciences the questionnaire as the foundation of research and very simple mathematical techniques (adding up in columns and percentages) by way of interpretative method. That the questionnaire, designed (as in sociology) by the enquirer, had to be completed by him too, the person questioned being dead, did not matter, provided the questions were sensibly designed and the data available for filling in the boxes. Though

23. J. E. Neale, *Essays in Elizabethan History* (London: Jonathan Cape, 1958), pp. 225 ff.

Sir Lewis Namier, who first applied the technique to the history of Parliament, worked on his own, it could lead to the sort of collaborative structure characteristic of scientific history when Neale assigned the analysis of particular Parliaments to various students whose completed questionnaires and statistical breakdowns (called master's theses) then formed the foundation of his own synthesis in *The Elizabethan House of Commons* (London, 1949). The method was by stages applied to different periods, especially the early and late seventeenth century. Using these techniques, Namier demolished established views of eighteenth-century politics, and Neale demonstrated the dominance of an increasingly politicized gentry in the Elizabethan Lower House.

These were undoubted gains—moves to a fuller truth, and the substitution of head counting for mere guesswork. The subsequent fate, however, of both scholars' work points up the dangers of this social science method. For one thing, its success depends far too much on the nature of the questionnaire, which (it would seem, inescapably) will tend to direct the research which it is supposed to assist. Namier's analysis of M.P.s began by leaving out two things—the possibility that they might have thinking minds and the certainty that they actually spent working time in the House of Commons. Predictably there thus emerged a House composed of people seduced into membership by strictly material motives and not interested in their membership except inasmuch as it served causes external to the work of Parliament. Neale's questionnaire omitted to ask after the subject's religious affiliation, an embarrassing omission when Neale in due course came to believe that religious views played the largest part in determining behavior in Parliament; in addition, he "proved" the significance of an increasing number of better experienced gentlemen in the House by assuming that it formed the explanation for a

supposed rise in political weight which formed a further un-
questioned and unanalyzed assumption. Both these "traditional"
historians thus in measure offended against the canons of
good historical scholarship—Neale much more so than Namier
because the former used supposedly sophisticated methods to
underpin a general scheme hallowed by tradition rather than
investigation, whereas the latter at least tested traditional
concepts by his methods, and tested them to destruction. They
made their mistakes the more readily because they thought
they had found assurance in the borrowed technique and
failed to note the dangers involved in such borrowing. The
social science methods employed by them were designed to
analyze structure (static conditions) and were thus ill-equipped
to cope with the basic problem of history, that is, change
through time. Namier, or rather his followers, thus came to
impose on a whole century and more the results of what an
analysis of a few years had told them, while Neale had to
inject the effects of change uncritically into an analysis capable
only of spotting the conditions of a cross-section at stated
points of time.

I might add that these once much-vaunted methods proved
particularly futile where most might have been expected of
them—in the study of that Parliament which divided into
warring parties and civil war in the seventeenth century.[24]
The criteria examined could discover no meaningful pointers
to the choice made by members except a small difference in
age. After all that laborious assembling of biographies and
all that careful construction of tables and percentages, we
still had no idea what it was that made some people fight

24. D. Brunton and D. H. Pennington, *Members of the Long Parliament*
(Cambridge: Cambridge University Press, 1954); Mary F. Keeler, *The Long
Parliament, 1640–1641: A Biographical Study of its Members* (Philadelphia:
American Philosophical Society, 1954).

for the king and some against him. We were back with the
methods of traditional history at its least social-scientific—
and I may perhaps claim that these old-fashioned methods
(studying all the evidence without preconceived assumptions)
have since then revolutionized the history of Neale's Parliaments,
solved many of the problems of the seventeenth-century Parliaments which social analysis could not penetrate, and removed
Namier's dictatorial hand from the eighteenth century.[25]

It will be answered that this ineffective borrowing from the
social sciences proves little. The scientific method lacked so-
phistication, even perhaps science, and the borrowers lacked
common sense. This would be much too severe a judgment.
The methods were at the time much favored by social scientists

25. I have in mind the "revisionist" case touching the history of Parliament
in the sixteenth to eighteenth centuries (cf. above, n. 16). For the sixteenth
century, this shows that the House of Commons did not "rise" in power,
restores the House of Lords to its proper position of eminence, and stresses
the need to concentrate on the main business of parliamentary meetings,
legislation (which required agreement), rather than the occasional political
squabbles. (See in particular G. R. Elton, "Parliament in the Sixteenth Century:
Function and Fortunes," *Historical Journal* 22 [1979]: 225 ff., and Sheila
Lambert, "Procedure in the House of Commons in the Early Stuart Period,"
English Historical Review 95 [1980]: 753 ff.) For the early Stuarts, revision
has done away with such hallowed notions as the constant and growing
conflict between Crown and Commons or the existence of a consistent opposition
on constitutional grounds; the unconvincing counterattacks (e.g., T. K. Rabb
and Derek Hirst in *Past and Present* 92 [1981]: 55–99), though they try to
reassert old views and do not present any serious new research, at least do
not cite "authority" for their resistance to revision. In the eighteenth century,
G. S. Holmes (*British Politics in the Reign of Anne* [London: Macmillan, 1967])
and W. A. Speck (*Tory and Whig: The Struggle in the Constituencies 1701–
15* [London: Macmillan, 1970]) repelled the invasion of mechanically Namierite
assaults on the reign of Queen Anne; and Namier's own work on the mid-
century has now been convincingly modified by J. C. D. Clark's study, *The
Dynamics of Change: The Crisis of the 1750s and English Party Systems* (Cambridge: Cambridge University Press, 1982). All these revisions owe nothing
to innovations in method but everything to independent thought backed by
the rigorous application of traditional methods. And there is a lot more of
this to come.

themselves, and whatever may be true of Neale, Namier possessed a powerful and original intelligence. To me it seems
rather that faith in methods overcame two things essential to
success at this game: a proper regard for the concerns of
history, which has to go beyond analysis and pattern to the
particular story, and an informed understanding of the nature
of historical enquiry. (Namier had no sort of training as an
historian, and Neale belonged to that pragmatic tradition that
refused to reflect upon the work in which it was engaged.)
In consequence they never worked out how to control the
usefulness of what they borrowed by the critiques of historical
reason and especially fell victims to the structuralist and functional errors much current at the time, which contemptuously
relegated the real study of change to the hands of the chronicler
and journalist.

Still, no doubt the methods were not very sophisticated and
would be ridiculed nowadays by any half-competent cliometrician. The second area of parliamentary studies invaded
by the new science tried rather harder to absorb the instructions
of the mentor. This area comprehended the behavior of M.P.s
in the House of Commons, more particularly the analysis of
voting behavior. I must here confess to some prejudice against
this supposedly revealing sort of enquiry. Ever since I heard
a very distinguished political scientist, condescendingly assured
that the techniques of his psephological science could, by
manipulating roll calls, improve the historian's analysis of
party formation, admit that to him the numerical vote cast
and not the contents of the motion voted on held any significance, I have had some difficulty in believing that the way
to salvation lies there. And the only serious study of the English
Parliament here relevant—W. O. Aydelotte's analysis, with the
aid of some complex statistical techniques, of voting behavior
in the House of Commons in the 1840s—increases my skep-

ticism: after decades of labor, we still await a comprehensive
answer, while provisional statements tend to confirm obvious
and well-known points.[26] Active work on the relatively few
division lists surviving for the seventeenth and eighteenth centuries has also produced less than world-shaking results.[27]
The input of labor seems altogether disproportionate to the
gain.

No doubt there is always some virtue in having the obvious
and well known proved by another method, but not much.
Here, too, the trouble would seem to arise from the same
causes that hampered the work influenced by the sociological
method of multibiographical analysis. The method is applied
by borrowing rather than by adaptation, so that the questions
are external to the evidence and do not naturally arise from
it, and the exercise ignores too many basic principles of historical
understanding. Thus, studying party structure in Parliament
from division lists (roll calls) overlooks the fact that divisions
were the only occasions on which members had to say yea
or nay to an issue, the more so because the old House of
Commons physically made abstention impossible to any member present during a division. The jump from the peculiar
conditions of a division to a general assessment of attitudes
and behavior requires techniques not allowed for in the model.

A third sector of parliamentary studies has attempted to
benefit from scientific techniques: an enterprise is in progress
which analyzes eighteenth-century poll-books (records of votes
cast in parliamentary elections) with the aid of the computer.

26. Aydelotte has put out a number of preliminary articles, especially "The
House of Commons in the 1840s," *History* 39 (1954): 249 ff., and "Voting
Patterns in the House of Commons in the 1840s," *Comparative Studies in
Society and History* 5 (1962–63): 134 ff. However, he tells me that he now
expects to finish the work before very long.

27. E.g., D. A. Rubini, "Party and the Augustan Constitution, 1694–1716,"
Albion 10 (1978): 193–208.

I would not wish to judge work well outside my own range
which remains unfinished and has not yet been subjected to
critical assessment by others. For the present it is clear that
the method makes possible analytical results not obtainable
in other ways, but it is far from clear that the interpretative
"model" applied to the data has allowed for the actual structure
of electorates and the possible motives behind the changes
documented.[28]

Coexistence among the Historians

The history of Parliament is peculiar, and many aspects of it
render cliometric influences particularly unsuitable. The fact,
however, underlines what has already been said: "scientific"
history cannot replace the various forms here housed together
in the "traditional" mansions and should entertain no such
ambition. For most of the questions with which traditional
history has commonly been concerned it serves very little purpose. Like most innovations in the history of historical studies,
it fulfills its true function best when it adds to the techniques
available for the analysis of historical evidence, mainly in order
that problems which previous historians could not or would
not study may become subject to historical enquiry. In this
respect it does not differ in essence from earlier such break-
throughs, though I am willing to believe that it might have
more formidable effects and even come within hailing distance
of the claims sometimes made for it. The science of paleography

28. W. A. Speck and W. A. Gray, "Computer Analysis of Poll Books: An
Initial Report," *Bulletin of the Institute of Historical Research* 43 (1970): 105–
12; the same with R. Hopkinson, "Computer Analysis of Poll Books; A Further
Report," ibid. 48 (1975): 64–90. For drawing attention to possible lines of
criticism—highly technical in respect of the sources but pretty convincing—
I am indebted to an unpublished paper by Dr. J. C. D. Clark.

and diplomatic (the handwriting and structure of documents), an achievement of the seventeenth century, opened up the real meaning of materials previously uncomprehended and therefore little used; it also made possible a much more refined testing of authenticity. Together with the antiquaries' interest in "relics," those technical innovations expanded historical interests from bare political narrative into investigations of topics often thought to be novel today: institutions, laws, ideas, social customs. The philological achievements of the eighteenth century introduced both a new rigor into documentary analysis and removed anachronistic interpretations of terms whose meaning had changed in time. The biological and anthropological work of the nineteenth century taught historians important lessons about developments and relativity in both facts and values. And so the story of influence and borrowing goes on: historians have rightly always been eager to use the latest methods.

In all these cases, positive benefits accrued largely by the opening up of additional areas of enquiry and by refining the analysis, but they were matched by dangers frequently overlooked at the time. The better analysis of documents could lead to blindness to the historical circumstances behind their production: its danger was mindless pedantry. Philology similarly caused historians to argue about meanings rather than events, and the history of ideas especially too readily became a history of words. Biology, especially after Darwin, produced a horrible crop of "evolutions" in history which endowed human institutions with personified identities and life cycles alien to their reality; it powerfully reinforced the so-called whiggish error of seeing all development as a march upward to improvement. And anthropology, so often a truly worthy instructor, still troubles the historian who follows its ways too loyally by

depriving him of the power to move from one state to another:
it tends to impose its own, essentially static, stance.[29]

What then are the gains to be expected from the *new* science
in history, and what dangers may it carry along with itself?
As Fogel emphasizes, its achievements lie in two areas—in
the study of long-term trends and developments and in a
more soundly based investigation of broad phenomena like
the economic effects of slavery or the demographic fortunes
of whole populations than was possible by traditional and
often impressionistic means. These constitute very notable
claims for attention. Where the right materials exist (a res-
ervation which excludes much history before 1700 and virtually
all history before 1500) the use of social science models, tested
by empirical data subjected to very sophisticated mathematical
treatment, offers an opportunity to arrive at reasonably well
grounded analyses of such things as population and family
history, the causes and effects of economic change, the history
of disease and death, of migration and of public finance. Very
creditable achievements indeed, and no sensible historian will
deny that the increase in knowledge provided, especially on
topics which earlier methods could not tackle at all successfully,
is a great gain. None of us will ever again talk quite so airily
about demographic change or fluctuations in the standard of
living as in the past we have done.

But "scientific" history, like all history, must claim neither
absolute rule nor even absolute superiority over other forms
of the discipline; indeed, until it acquires a language accessible
to the generality, it can scarcely demand equality. Its weaknesses
strike one as quite commensurate to its strengths. Despite

29. Even so excellent a book as Keith Thomas's *Religion and the Decline
of Magic* (London: Weidenfeld & Nicolson, 1970), which uses anthropology
most judiciously, never really gets *going* over the two hundred years it covers:
it tends to circle around a succession of static situations.

attempts to deny this, it can effectively operate only by suppressing the individual—by reducing its subject matter to a collectivity of human data in which the facts of humanity have real difficulty in surviving. Even those cliometricians who recognize (as some do not) the importance of detail cannot by their methods operate with this detail unless they abstract particularity from it. Cliometrics therefore serves the history of mankind quite admirably when that history is seen as one of concepts and structures, but it is markedly less useful when that history turns to the story of people.

Secondly, like all analyses which apply the model technique, cliometrics always faces the danger that its arguments become self-validating. Models do dictate the terms of reference, define the parameters, direct the research, and thus are very liable to pervert the search for empirical evidence by making it selective. There are ways of guarding against this, especially the insistence that all the available evidence be used, but since in history even all the available evidence never amounts to a totality (no series is ever complete) the possibility that the model may be used to fill the gaps always arises. The danger is by no means peculiar to scientific history, though in traditional history model-users are not even always aware that they are employing that technique.[30] One would feel happier if those

30. Neale proved the existence of a puritan opposition in the Elizabethan House of Commons by positing it (making it his model) and then reading all his evidence in the light of that postulate. Hill has always operated with a basically Marxist class model of seventeenth-century developments in which the slot of the variable (the revolutionary) has got successively filled by the bourgeoisie, the lesser gentry, the artisans ("industrious sort"), and lastly by no particular group, in spite of which lapse the model remained in being: a bourgeois revolution has become a revolution, expressly not made by a bourgeoisie, in which benefits accrue to what have in advance been defined as bourgeois values and aspirations (this is the burden of his argument in *Change and Continuity in Seventeenth-Century England* [London: Weidenfeld & Nicolson, 1974], pp. 278–84). The history of labor and labor movements

models were derived from a study of the evidence and not
borrowed from supposedly scientific work in the social sciences—if, that is, historical method were allowed to control
the borrowing.

Thirdly, like all previous historians aiming at "science,"
cliometricians are always in danger of regarding their results
as a good deal more certain and established than they are.
The method is so mathematical that it produces a false sense
of security. This danger is aggravated by any desire to discover
the laws of human behavior. If one believes that the study of
the past can produce laws with predictive power one cannot
allow for the possibility that one's conclusions are debatable
or tentative. However, the violent controversies among cliometricians indicate that the new methods provide more opportunities for disagreement and indeed abuse than the sort
of consensus that one might suppose scientific procedure would
ensure. The fact is that, being applied to very large and at
times very tenuous themes, cliometric methods, though superior
to mere impressionism, are a great deal less secure and conclusive than old-fashioned methods based on the trained study
of historical evidence and applied to the more sharply defined
problems thus investigated. What cliometrics has so far produced is an opening up of areas of uncertainty in major and
important topics. As for all that lawmaking (not, so far as I
can see, practiced by a careful cliometrician like Fogel), one

---

is dominated by rarely examined models; so, until not so long ago, was that
of aristocracy and gentry. The history of crime in England has been bedeviled
by a class model of behavior—the notion that the criminal law existed solely
to protect the ascendancy of the ruling order; a good example for this mistaken
view is found in Douglas Hay, "Property, Authority and the Criminal Law,"
in *Albion's Fatal Tree*, ed. Hay and others (London: A. Lane, 1975), pp. 17
ff. For an attack on this model, see John H. Langbein, "*Albion's* Fatal Flaws,"
Past and Present 98 (1983): 96–120. The dominance of this model has generally
rendered historians incapable of accounting for the empirically well established
fact that thieves attacked the poor far more than they did the rich.

might think that past experience would cure people of this age-old ambition; but the desire suits certain idealistic and positive temperaments among progressive intellectuals and will thus continue to operate. This is particularly true of the United States, where the old faith that man can direct his own destiny has become transmuted into the belief that man in the mass can be told by the social scientist what his fate will be. So long as no one takes all these laws seriously the harm will be small; as Marxist regimes have proved to our generation, the harm becomes total when the confident theories of social science historians turn into a doctrine defended by the power of the state.

"Scientific" historians, riding a well-deserved crest, need to beware of arrogance, as indeed Fogel, distinguished even among them, himself takes pains to explain to them. Arrogance is not proof of achievement but rather a sign of inner unease— and that unease they need no longer feel. "Traditional" historians need to beware of bigotry—a bigotry induced by the sense of a threat to their shaky ascendancy. And yet that threat never existed because "ascendancy" was always the wrong word for the relations of colleagues. All good historians are traditional historians because they observe the traditions of a profession dedicated to the unbiased study of the past, conscious of the unending variety of that past and the great variety of techniques which help that study, and well aware that however far they advance they will never come to a final conclusion.

CONCLUSION

W e conclude as we began, by emphasizing that our two papers are offered not as methodological writs, but as personal commentaries on prevailing practices among working historians. We have not tried to conceal the respect that each of us has for the other's work, although we hasten to add that this mutual appreciation has grown bit by bit over the years. Our first encounter was at a conference organized by *History and Theory* in the spring of 1968 where we were expected to represent methodological extremes and did not entirely disappoint our sponsors. During the ensuing years we pursued quite different research interests, but we read each other's work and we continued to discuss the diverse methodological practices and prescriptions in our discipline. Because we approached history with greatly differing backgrounds (one trained as an economist in the age of econometrics and mathematical models; the other trained as a Tudor historian at London University at a time when medievalists who concentrated on studying the details of particular documents were highly influential), the potential for remaining antagonists was great. Yet reading and dialogue led each of us to a more ecumenical view than we were originally prepared to entertain.

Our essays reveal not only mutual respect and common views, but continuing differences on important points. Fogel, for example, is far more sanguine than Elton on the usefulness and scope of social-scientific models in historical research. Elton points to the capacity of flashy models to blind historians and to instances in which such blindness has led to ridiculous conclusions. Fogel points to instances in which models have led historians to unsuspected bodies of evidence or extracted more evidence from known sources than had previously been thought possible. Elton stresses that too many social science models are spun out of the air and are imposed on historical situations in such a way as to distort reality. Fogel stresses the pitfalls of implicit theorizing which smuggles untenable assumptions into apparently straightforward narratives.

If nothing else, such point and counterpoint reveals that neither traditional nor cliometric methods are free of pitfalls. It also raises the question of whether these pitfalls are inherent in the method or arise from inept applications of the method. It is not surprising that we have offered somewhat different answers to this question. Each wants the other to judge the methodology he advocates by its best rather than its worst applications. Each is suspicious of the other's claim that an admittedly poor application of his preferred method should be attributed to the ineptness of a hapless practitioner rather than to inherent limitations in that method. We also differ on how to define "scientific" and "traditional" history. Fogel based the definitions on his view of the central tendency of actual practices within the two groups. Elton's redefinition of "traditional" history is based on his view of "best" practices, which excludes certain categories of actual work on the ground that they are bad history.

Given the importance of these and other points of disagreement, some readers may doubt our opening claim that we agree on methodological matters "far more than we disagree." Yet that claim seems quite justified to us. Even though we have different views of the range of issues to which social science methods may be productively applied, we often agree on whether a particular application of these methods constitutes good or bad history. Even though we differ on how to define "traditional" history, we are quite close in our views of which of the works under contention are good history and which ones are bad history. In other words we believe that there are standards of quality against which all historical work ought to be judged.

Of all of the elements that affect the quality of an historical work, none is more important than the thoroughness of the search for evidence and the care that is taken in the investigation of the provenance, domain, and reliability of the evidence. We take issue with those who argue that details are subordinate to interpretation, not because we celebrate facts for their own sake, but because the quality of an historical interpretation is critically dependent on the quality of the details out of which it is spun. Time and again the interpretation of major historical events, sometimes of whole areas, has been transformed by the correction of apparently trivial details—by the demonstration that the authorship of a document, the exact sequence of a series of bills or amendments, the course of the prices of a commodity, the level of inventories, the size of a population, or some other detail initially treated as "mere" background information had been erroneously reported.

There are some historians who lose themselves in details, piling fact upon fact without adding to our understanding of the historical events to which the facts pertain. What is needed, of course, is a proper balance between evidence and interpretation. History is itself an historical phenomenon which evolves in a complex way. At this particular point in the history of history the main problem is not that there is a superabundance of effort devoted to the accumulation of facts but that there is a superabundance of effort devoted to the search for new interpretations of the existing, often exceedingly sparse, corpus of evidence. Much of the current output of bad history takes the form of elaborate interpretations of meager sets of "stylized" facts which, if correct, would not bear the weight that is placed on them. Moreover, the "stylized" facts are

often such superficial or erroneous characterizations of the
past that even the correction of the errors is relatively
unproductive.

The tendency to subordinate facts to theory has been pro-
moted by the view that each age rewrites the history of the
past because the values and interests of historians are conditioned by the values and interests of their age. That much
of the current work has been spawned in this way is beyond
doubt. Surely the explosion of research in such fields as black
history, women's history, the history of various Third World
nations, the history of the family, and urban history have been
stimulated by the experience and problems of our age. But
changes in ideology are not necessarily the only, or even the
primary, inspiration for the rewriting of history. Many recent
reinterpretations of old questions have come about because
these questions have been more thoroughly investigated by
the new generation of scholars than by their predecessors.
Such advances have usually been based on the exploitation of
new sources of evidence or of known sources that were too
large or too complex to have been of much use at earlier
points in the development of the historical arts. It is certainly
true that many of the bodies of evidence currently exploited
by cliometricians and many of their challenges to traditional
interpretations had to await the development of high-speed
computers. The revolution in Tudor history, much of which
is based on the establishment of the provenance of particular
documents and the proper ordering of various bills and
amendments was, if not made possible, at least facilitated by
the calendaring of the letters and papers of Henry VIII.

The current tendency to subordinate the search for facts to
the search for new interpretations tends to impoverish both,
since this approach fails to exploit the symbiotic relationship
between these two aspects of history. The enrichment of the

evidential base not only strengthens the foundation for previous historical interpretations; it frequently leads to more numerous, more surprising, and more far-reaching new interpretations than are produced by intensive efforts to rethink old but patchy evidence. Although we work on widely different problems and exploit different types of evidence, we have both benefited enormously from unexpected issues tossed up by the evidence.

When Elton rediscovered Thomas Cromwell, some scholars maintained that because he was living in an era of administrative ascendancy and because he represented a tory point of view that emphasized administrative action and control, Elton had sought Cromwell out and had made a hero of him. The way in which Elton actually came across Cromwell was quite different. Because his postgraduate research was focused on Henry VIII, Elton started reading the calendar of papers for Henry's reign. Since his mind was quite sufficiently stocked with the conventional history disseminated by Pollard and others, Cromwell was not a figure that loomed large in Elton's thought. Yet he kept coming across the name of Cromwell, which was barely mentioned in any of the history books of the day. The oddity could hardly have been overlooked. Cromwell seemed to lead to everything and yet no one had seen or acknowledged his role. Elton took up the study of Cromwell, not because he wanted to find a maker of the state, a bureaucrat, but because Cromwell loomed so large in the evidence. Elton did not go looking for Cromwell; Cromwell sought him out.

Before he became interested in the relative efficiency of slave and free labor in southern agriculture, Fogel had little interest in the demography of slaves or of any other population. He was led into demographic issues as a result of efforts to obtain better measures of the labor of slaves in the production of cotton. One aspect of the problem concerned the amount of time that women were absent from field work because of pregnancy and the nursing of infants. While searching for evidence on this question, he came across lists prepared by slaveholders which gave the ages of slave mothers and of all of their surviving children. These lists showed that the age of mothers at the birth of the oldest child was several years greater than convention dictated and called into question the prevailing views on a wide range of issues, including the importance of slave breeding in the profitability of slavery and the nature of the sexual mores of slaves.[1]

One of the unanticipated by-products of the debate on slave demography was the discovery that data on physical height could be used to establish the age of menarche and the level of nutrition, issues that were provoked by the contention that the late age of first birth had no bearing on slave mores but merely reflected the late age at which slave women became menarchial and the poor state of their nutrition. This discovery and the abundance of data on height for various North American and European populations (which stretch back to the beginning of the eighteenth century) have stimulated a number of comparative studies of the course of nutrition, labor productivity, and labor welfare. Although still relatively new, this work is leading to unanticipated revisions and amendments of prevailing views on the consequences of the Industrial Revolution, on the determinants of the vital revolution, and on other issues

1. As it turned out, the problem of making valid inferences of the age of mothers at their first birth from this body of data was more complex than Fogel had initially realized, but even the pursuit of such technical statistical issues proved to be fruitful for research on other historical problems. Cf. James Trussell and Richard Steckel, "The Age of Slaves at Menarche and Their First Birth," *Journal of Interdisciplinary History* 8 (1978): 477–505, and Robert W. Fogel, "Circumstantial Evidence in 'Scientific' and Traditional History," in *Philosophy of History and Contemporary Historiography*, ed. David Carr et al. (Ottawa: Ottawa University Press, 1982), pp. 90–93.

far removed from the relative efficiency of slave agriculture in the antebellum South.

"There are more things in heaven and earth," Hamlet said to Horatio, "than are dreamt of in your philosophy." The conviction that unites us, one that transcends whatever differences we still have on the role of social-scientific methods, is that there are far more things in historical evidence than are embodied in current interpretations of history. The search for these things is the challenge that we hope will fire the imagination of those about to embark on the study of history.

INDEX

ad hominem arguments, 46, 50, 54, 87, 98, 103, 104
Adams, George Burton, 10
Adams, Henry, 10
Adams, Herbert Baxter, 15
American Historical Association, 10, 21n
American Liberty League, 13
analogical argument, 31, 50, 93, 95–97
Annales E.S.C., annalistes, 17, 75
Anne, Queen of England, 113n
anthropology, 9, 18, 31, 61, 81, 117, 118n. *See also* social sciences and history
approximation. *See* probability and approximation
authority, argument by. *See* ad hominem arguments
Aydelotte, W. O., 114, 115 and n

Barker, Richard, 94, 95
Beard, Charles, 12, 13, 18, 58
Becker, Carl, 12, 13
Beecher Stowe, Harriet, 45, 84, 85
behavioral laws. *See* laws, social and historical; models
bias (in historical research and writing). *See* objectivity and bias
biology, 9, 10, 61, 117
Bloch, Marc, 18
Braudel, Fernand, 19, 20, 31, 41, 75 and n, 109
Burgess, John William, 11

California Institute of Technology, 39
Cambridge Group for the History of Population and Social Structure, 34, 35, 61, 63, 107
Cambridge University, 3, 75n, 109n

Carnegie-Mellon University, 39
Carr, Edward H., 102n, 103n
circumstantial evidence. *See* evidence, historical
Clark, J. C. D., 113n
class history. *See* history, marxist approach to
cliometrics, cliometricians, 2, 23–33, 37–41, 44, 45, 50–54, 56, 57, 60–65, 67–69, 74, 77, 81, 82, 84, 89, 99, 103, 105–07, 110, 116, 119, 120. *See also* economic history; demography; quantitative history; "scientific" history; family history; political history; parliamentary history; urban history
collectivities and individuals, 20, 29, 32, 33, 41–44, 69, 76, 77, 79, 83. *See also* generalization and general laws; laws, social and historical
Collingwood, R. G., 12
computer, use of, 2, 51, 52, 115, 126
Conrad, Alfred H., 36, 51
Croce, Benedetto, 12
Cromwell, Thomas, 58, 127
cultural warfare, 7, 65, 70

Darwin, Charles, 10, 117
data, historical. *See* historical facts; evidence, historical; sources, historical
demography, demographic history, 9, 23, 48, 61, 63, 80, 82, 110, 118, 127, 128
Dilthey, Wilhelm, 12
diplomatics, 9, 117
documents. *See* sources, historical; evidence, historical
Droysen, Johann Gustav, 11, 12, 50n, 96n

131

U. S.: historical practice in, (*continued*)
17, 18, 28, 32, 33, 35–37, 44, 50, 55, 58, 59, 69, 127–29
University of Chicago: Economic History Workshop, 63
University of Michigan, 40; Inter-University Consortium for Political and Social Research, 52
Uppsala University, 63
urban history, 24, 110, 126

Vann Woodward, C., 18

verification. *See* evidence, historical (verification and evaluation of)
Vico, Giambattista, 16
Vinson, Fred M., 15

Washington, George, 32
women, history of, 59, 99, 126
World War I, 16
Wrigley, E. A., 22, 23

Zeisel, Hans, 21, 22